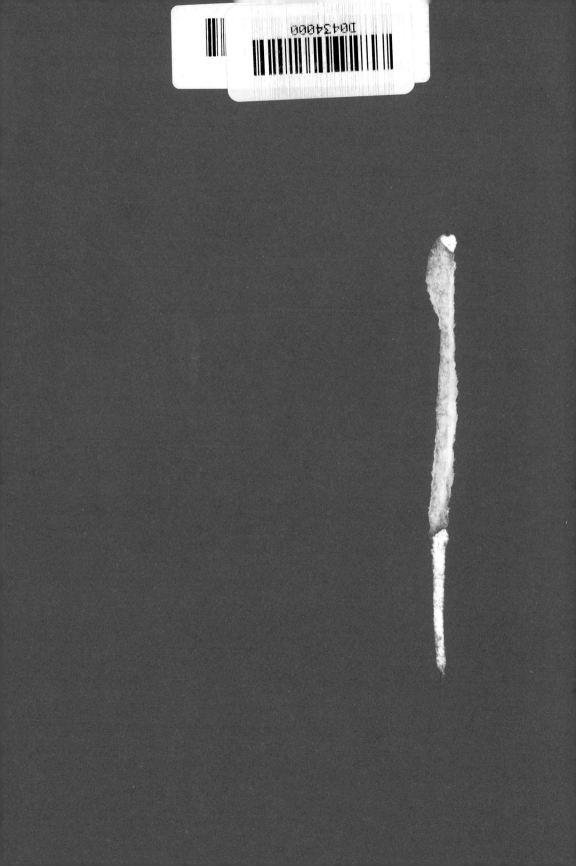

natural
Cat Care

natural
Cat Care

Christopher Day

hamlyn

To my long-suffering family and to my
many noble and enigmatic patients.

An Hachette UK Company
www.hachette.co.uk

First published in Great Britain in 2011 by
Hamlyn, a division of Octopus Publishing Group Ltd
Endeavour House
189 Shaftesbury Avenue
London
WC2H 8JY
www.octopusbooks.co.uk

ISBN: 978-0-600-62117-1

A CIP catalogue record for this book is available
from the British Library

Printed and bound in China

10 9 8 7 6 5 4 3 2 1

Note Unless the information is specific to males or
females, throughout this book kittens and cats are
referred to as 'she' and the information and advice
are applicable to both sexes.

The advice in this book is provided as general
information only. It is not necessarily specific
to any individual case and is not a substitute for
the guidance and advice provided by a licensed
veterinary practitioner consulted in any particular
situation. Octopus Publishing Group accepts no
liability or responsibility for any consequences
resulting from the use of or reliance upon the
information contained herein. No cats were
harmed in the making of this book.

CONTENTS

INTRODUCTION

Cats have overtaken dogs in popularity as household pets. They have a place in our homes and hearts almost as if they were part of the human family. These treasured companions and pets are comforting and healing members of our households.

When you bring a cat into your home, whether kitten or adult, you want her to have the best of everything to ensure her welfare and happiness for a long and healthy life. When you take on a cat, you also take on a responsibility and duty of care. Of course, your vet is the first port of call, should anything go wrong with your cat's health, but it is more constructive to think in terms of positive health and prevention of disease through establishing a healthy lifestyle and environment for your cat as the most effective insurance against illness.

While modern Western medicine has much to offer, ill health is still prevalent. In the USA, an estimated 450 cats per 100,000 develop cancer each year. Arthritis, autoimmune disease, asthma, allergy, urinary problems, skin problems, thyroid disease, diabetes and other chronic diseases blight the lives of so many of our beloved feline companions. It is clear that all is not well, despite the heavy investment in veterinary research and the development of modern medicines.

No wonder then that more attention has been focused in recent times on natural and holistic lifestyle approaches for our family and for animals. There is a great deal of logic behind the notion that, if our cats were to eat more healthily, drink good water and enjoy a lifestyle as free from stress as possible and that allows behavioural needs to be fulfilled, their health and resistance to disease are likely to be better. If we also restrict their exposure to chemicals and, should their health begin to waver, use gentle natural medicine techniques to stimulate the body into regaining health, we avoid the risk of adverse drug effects, unless they become absolutely necessary to maintain welfare or to preserve life itself.

This book is designed to help the caring owner to encourage positive health and to establish routines for better health and welfare. It has often been said that prevention is better than cure. Certainly, it is preferable to plan your daily routines to do as much as you can to prevent illness and to avoid the need for veterinary intervention. However, this book is not designed to act as a substitute for proper veterinary care in the event of disease or illness. A visit to your vet for diagnosis and assessment is recommended whenever your cat becomes ill. If you are lucky enough to have a vet in the neighbourhood who is trained both in modern conventional medicine and holistic and natural medicine, so much the better, since all medical options can then be considered and an objective and balanced medical programme devised.

This book is a compact introduction to the options available, and necessarily does not pretend to be a complete treatise. It offers a guide to a more natural lifestyle for your cat and provides a practical pointer to natural medicine options.

YOU AND YOUR CAT
ABOUT CATS

The domestic cat (*Felis silvestris catus*) is thought to have descended from the wild Desert Cat of North Africa (*Felis silvestris lybica*), possibly as a result of human intervention. Believed to have been a cult animal in ancient Egypt, the cat has been associated with human settlements for about ten thousand years and is now the most numerous 'pet' species in the world.

Domestic cats have descended from the wild Desert Cat of North Africa.

HOW CATS BECAME DOMESTICATED

The process of domestication is likely to have been initiated by cats frequenting human dwellings as a ready source of food and shelter and, because of our tendency to leave food scraps around, mice also became readily available as prey. Cats are not inherently scavengers and their natural food sources are small birds and small rodents, although stronger individuals have been known to kill and eat prey as large as pigeons and rabbits.

THE NATURE OF CATS

All domestic cats belong to the one species, whose evolutionary origins do much to explain the nature of the species. Cats are loosely social animals, with a tendency to live in colonies that have a recognized hierarchy, and can be fiercely territorial. They tend to hunt alone, but bring food back to the colony for those less well able to hunt, for instance a nursing mother that would not be able to provide well for her young during the first few days after giving birth. However, cats don't tend to show pack behaviour or 'pay homage' to a leader, unlike their distant lion relations.

Cats are obligate carnivorous animals, which means that they require meat and material derived from animal carcasses as a source of nutrients. Furthermore, this food should be fresh, since cats are prone to food poisoning. They are patient and stealthy hunters with excellent stalking ability and acute vision, and are capable of nocturnal activity. Cats are able to catch, hold, kill and dismember prey carcasses, ranging in size from mice up to rabbit-sized birds and mammals. They also eat insects, reptiles and amphibians, and have the ability to chew the bones of small prey. Plant material is mostly obtained from the ingested matter of their prey. Having desert origins, the healthy cat is very economical with water.

In the domesticated context, cats can be extremely companionable, providing a great deal of comfort to their human housemates. However, a cat also likes to have its own life, and doesn't aspire to serve mankind in the manner of, say, a dog. The diversity of colour, coat length and texture, shape and size of modern domestic cats has been created by man's experiment and curiosity. This diversity is mostly driven by a quest for different outward appearance rather than to serve any particular domestic purpose or service, unlike in the development of dog breeds.

MATING AND BREEDING HABITS

When breeding, female cats give birth to a number of temporarily blind, defenceless and dependent young, called a litter, which then suckle from their (normally ten) mammary glands and teats. In addition to providing milk, mother cats regurgitate food for their young until the kittens become less dependent. A female cat of breeding age, known as a 'queen', is able to delay ovulation when she is 'on heat' (in oestrus) until she finds a suitable mate, and can be 'calling' – another term for being on heat – for prolonged periods of time. A cat's gestation period is about nine weeks in duration.

BREEDS AND THEIR CHARACTERISTICS

Short-haired

Abyssinian a lithe and well-muscled cat, with a distinctively 'ticked' coat

British Blue the most popular variant of the British Shorthair, this cat enjoys a 'quiet life'

Burmese with European and American variants, this oriental breed is very sociable and intelligent

Burmilla with origins in the Chinchilla and Burmese, was bred for coat and an amenable, sociable disposition

Cornish Rex/Devon Rex Rex cats have been bred with a curly or wavy coat, whether light or thick

Egyptian Mau the only naturally spotted cat, close to the Desert Cat of North Africa

Manx tails are of varying length from 'tail-less' to normal in this cat

Siamese an oriental breed, known for its voice and for its coloured 'points'

Long-haired

Angora an ancient Turkish breed with a medium-length silky white coat

Birman the so-called 'Sacred Cat of Burma' with a pale coat, dark points and deep blue eyes

Maine Coon an intelligent, gentle and very large cat

Persian a long-haired cat typically with a short face

Ragdoll with a colourpoint coat and blue eyes, this breed is relaxed and sociable

Turkish Van this cat has a white coat and coloured head and tail and enjoys water

ABOUT KITTENS

During kittenhood so many physical, behavioural and health patterns become established, hence the extreme importance of careful holistic rearing. Play between littermates starts to unfold a cat's instinctive behaviour, and the mother will also teach certain behaviour responses and life skills. Since this phase is vital to the social development of the adult, a kitten should not be removed from her mother before eight weeks of age.

The mother teaches her young litter the life skills and behaviour necessary for survival.

EARLY DEVELOPMENT

Kittens are born after about nine weeks of pregnancy. The mother normally bites the navel cord to liberate the tiny, sightless but avidly hungry kitten, which actively seeks out a nipple, wrestling with her littermates in her fight for food.

After about 12 days, the eyes open to give the kitten limited vision. Her visual needs at this stage are restricted to the nest area.

Sight develops progressively, as does independence. The skeleton is very soft and pliable at first, being composed mainly of cartilage until ossification gradually turns cartilage to bone during the kitten's subsequent growth and development.

WEANING AND TEETHING

A kitten is able to deal with regurgitated meat or meat scrapings from an early age.

The 26 deciduous or milk teeth erupt from the third week of life, which will eventually irritate the mother during nursing so that weaning can commence. However, it is not until the full complement of (normally) 30 adult teeth develops, between four to seven months of age, that the kitten can deal really effectively with chunks of raw meat and bones. If you plan to feed your kitten a natural diet, then it is important that she is given bones and meat during her early development, in order to learn the necessary skills and habits for safely applying such a diet. It is usual for a young kitten to want to chew, especially during periods of teething. You can satisfy this need by providing bones and chunks of meat, thus saving damage to furniture, fittings and clothing in the process and preventing the subsequent friction between human and cat that may occur as a consequence of such damage. This may also offset the attraction of electric cables, which seem to be endlessly fascinating to a teething kitten and pose the risk of serious injury or death.

PLAYING SAFE

When playing with a young kitten, it is important to remember that her milk teeth are very sharp. If there are young children in the household, you must ensure that they are supervised when interacting with the kitten, so that both child and kitten can learn how to play sociably and safely together.

It is important when picking up a kitten to take great care not to drop her. A kitten can display incredible escapology skills, making it difficult to hold her safely. While the kitten is discovering her home environment, it is vital

Play is formative for a cat's skills, behaviour and development.

that you take careful precautions with doors in the house and also around and in the car, in order to avoid injury. Kittens and young cats are attracted by the warmth of a cooling car engine, and if the vehicle cannot be secured out of reach in a garage, they can hide under the bonnet (hood) or lie on the wheel under the wing (fender). Many kittens have been killed or maimed by the turning wheels or moving parts of a car engine, having climbed inside without the driver's knowledge. Many more have travelled long distances and become lost as a result of this tendency.

> **REMEMBER...**
> It is vital to ask your vet for a health check when you first take your kitten home or soon after, to look for any early signs of disease and developmental or congenital issues.

EXERCISE AND PLAY

It is essential that you provide your growing kitten with the opportunity for exercise and play in order to continue her education and socialization as well as to encourage a healthy heart and circulation, sound skeletal structure and muscular wellbeing. In fact, all a cat's life functions depend upon the challenge of exercise, which results in healthy development and maintenance.

Cats enjoy freedom, but are a danger to wild birds. They can be formidable hunters.

THE ROLE OF PLAY AND REST

Play is important for your kitten to learn about action and reaction, develop balance, distance judgement and poise, bond with the human family and maintain a healthy outlook on life. However, all kittens and adult cats require periods of quiet and rest during the day, so you need to provide your kitten or cat with a designated area in the home where she feels secure and children should be taught to respect her resting time.

It is important that you teach children to recognize the limits of playtime too. Playing with an energetic and fun-loving kitten can be so absorbing for children that it can be difficult for them to know when to stop. It is therefore vital that you supervise any such play until a safe routine has been established.

OUTDOOR ACTIVITIES

Although cats can generally gain enough opportunity for play and exercise indoors, some time spent outside is important for their mental and sensory stimulation. Some cats can even enjoy going for walks, like dogs. If your cat is to be allowed outside for any period of time, you will need to appreciate the potential toll on the local wildlife. Cats not only catch many small rodents classed as vermin, up to the size of rats, but are also very effective hunters of wild birds and other small creatures. It may be dangerous to tether or otherwise restrain a

Claws are exercised and sharpened on a soft surface, so it is better to provide a scratch pad.

cat out in the open, since it can be susceptible to attack by predators including foxes and birds of prey, but you can provide or construct an outdoor run for your cat.

Before allowing your cat to venture outdoors unattended, it is worth ensuring that your feline is familiar with the immediate vicinity so that she can easily find her way home. A cat should therefore be able to see out of a window and can be put outside in a basket for short spells before release.

You may find it worthwhile installing a cat flap, to allow your cat free access in or out of the home. Of course, if the family's cat can go in and out at will, so can a neighbour's cat. Depending on the particular design, cat flaps can be permanently unlocked, locked for certain times of the day or night or even controlled by a device on the cat's collar.

CLIMBING AND CLAWING

Cats love to climb and relax in high places, so it is essential to allow them this facility. They will also play for hours in discarded cardboard boxes. You can easily construct entertaining play areas by joining cardboard boxes together and cutting out doors, windows and tunnels for your cat's adventure and exploration.

Cats enjoy climbing in trees and may even take refuge in one when chased by a dog. Stories abound of worried owners seeking help to rescue a cat from a tree. However, cats are so agile that it is extremely unlikely that they will be in real need of rescue.

A cat's claws are retractable, a capability that requires regular exercise. It is advisable to provide a scratch pad, log or other object for this purpose, and for your cat to maintain the length and sharpness of her claws without savaging treasured furniture or fittings.

TRAINING

Cats may be independently minded, but most will respond to basic training and follow routines and schedules. You also need to make it clear what is acceptable behaviour and what is not. Your cat should at least be willing to submit to careful examination and handling so that this is not a source of great trauma to her in the event of treatment for injury or illness.

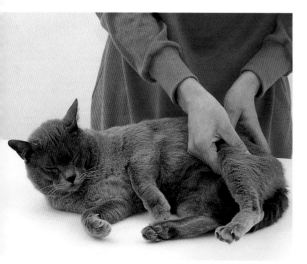

Teach your cat to enjoy the occasional mock 'examination'.

FEAR-FREE HANDLING

From early kittenhood it is a good idea to carry out a mock examination and handling of all parts of your pet's body including feet, claws, ears, teeth, mouth and under the tail to prevent any no-go areas being established. It is also worthwhile holding your kitten, carefully and gently, in many different positions. Strong-willed kittens may object to some part of this routine, but you need to

overcome this resistance with firmness, love and persistence to ensure that your kitten is comfortable or even enjoys this well-meaning attention. A kitten with no fear of being restrained, turned onto her back and having her mouth opened will be much happier at the veterinary clinic when the need for a visit arises. A cat should learn to play gently, especially if there are young children in the household, never biting or scratching.

TEACHING 'NO' AND 'COME'

Your cat understanding the word 'no' to mean that she should stop whatever she is doing may also be a potential life saver and will certainly make for better relationships with humans throughout her life. Always use the word 'no' firmly and clearly.

Cats tend to enjoy warmth and seek warm and comfortable places to lie, which may include in front of the cooker, especially if there is a mat or carpet in place and particularly if it is a range cooker that is kept warm throughout the day. While you may consider this behaviour tolerable, you need to be aware that it is a source of potential danger to human and animal alike if it obstructs safe access to the cooker or if hot pans are being held above the cat. Accidental spillage can cause serious burning or scalding injury. This is where the 'no' command can be put to effective use should you decide to discourage your cat from this behaviour.

A cat should come when called. You can usually establish this by allowing your cat freedom before a meal and then calling her for her food, which will serve as an encouraging reward for the behaviour.

HOUSE TRAINING

Toilet training comes naturally to most cats, and some individuals have even been known to teach themselves to use the human toilet. Providing your cat with access to a clean litter tray at all times will usually ensure that there is no soiling of the house. Inappropriate urination or defecation in the home can be a very distressing habit and stopping it can represent a real challenge. However, it is usually a behavioural response in your cat and

ON CATS' INDEPENDENCE...

It has often been said and is tacitly accepted that 'dogs have masters, cats have staff'. British author Rudyard Kipling painted a wonderful word picture of the cat in one of his Just So Stories, 'The Cat that Walked by Himself', in which the cat often repeats: 'I am the Cat who walks by himself, and all places are alike to me.'

homeopathic treatment can often resolve the problem (see pages 80–81).

FEEDING ISSUES

Cats can be fussy feeders. You can reduce this tendency by taking a matter-of-fact approach to feeding, in which food is put down and removed if not eaten. Leaving food down all day will only encourage your cat to be fussy and necessitates the feeding of dry foods to prevent the risk of food poisoning.

House cats should be encouraged to use a litter tray.

DAY-TO-DAY CARE
GROOMING

A wild cat grooms itself and maintains its claws, skin, teeth and coat in good condition. Domestic cats bred for certain characteristics, fed an unnatural diet or given unsuitable exercise can require special grooming attention. Cats with long coats or those with bad teeth require regular combing and brushing, since tangling or matting can lead to skin disease.

Regular grooming is vital for cats with long coats, as tangles and mats can lead to disease.

A POSITIVE EXPERIENCE

Your cat should enjoy her coat being groomed from the outset, but be careful not to strike any bony areas if using a metal comb. If you find grooming your cat difficult to carry out at

home, seek help from a professional cat groomer. Grooming may be combined with massage for extra benefit, and can be highly rewarding for both you and your cat (see page 59).

TOENAILS

The toenails of a cat that has plenty of exercise opportunity, including access to a scratch pad or tree, will usually remain healthy. However, some cats do require help in maintaining toenail length and condition, which can be due to either their advanced age or being physically unable to exercise properly. Vets are usually very willing to help with toenail care, but it is also something that can be done at home using a good-quality set of toenail clippers. It is important that your cat should not be hurt by the procedure by cutting too close to the 'quick' or pinching it, as she will then acquire an understandable extreme fear of having her nails clipped.

The claws can be revealed by gently squeezing from beneath the foot, with your thumb above the foot, and it is usually easy to

Choice of nail clipper is personal, but a clear view of the 'quick' is essential while clipping.

see the quick in pale claws. A cut should not be made closer than about 2 mm (1/16 in) from the tip of the quick and always from the dorsal to the ventral – the ground side to the upper side of the nail. Never make the cut from side to side, or painful pinching can result, even without drawing blood. If in doubt, veterinary help may be the wiser option. It is important to check all dewclaws, to reduce the risk of injury.

TEETH

A cat's teeth need to be subjected to the stresses and strains of chewing raw meat and bones to maintain healthy function, so feeding a natural diet of raw meat with occasional small raw bones to chew may prevent your cat having problems with its teeth and gums (see pages 18–19). Cats can be fussy eaters and many require dental attention because of starchy, dry or sloppy foods. Should tartar begin to develop, it must be cracked or scraped away before it causes gum disease and gum recession. Gum disease will threaten the longevity of the teeth and can lead to serious systemic disease, such as kidney problems. You can easily remove minor scaling by using your thumbnail, picking at the edge of the tartar nearest to the gum. If your cat already has bad oral health, you may need to ask a vet for help in order to gain a fresh start.

EARS

In most cats ears require no attention, but they should nonetheless be checked from time to time. Signs of trouble can include scratching or shaking the ears, the appearance of excessive wax or discharge and the affected ear being held low (see pages 72–73). If your cat suffers a skin problem, the ears may also be affected, resulting in inflammation, excess wax production or even pathological discharge (see pages 66–67). Veterinary help could be needed, but you may be able to obtain sufficient relief for your cat by using aromatherapy (see pages 52–53). In cats with generalized skin and ear problems, a homeopathic constitutional prescription should be sought from a holistic vet (see pages 48–51).

White cats are prone to skin tumours, particularly at the tip of the ear flap; you should seek veterinary advice if you note any scaling, crusting, inflammation or colour change in this area. Coconut oil can offer reasonable sun protection for such ears.

DAY-TO-DAY FEEDING

As the domestic cat's ancestor is the Desert Cat of North Africa, this creature's lifestyle and diet offers an informative guide when it comes to devising the optimum natural diet for your pet cat. However, if your cat is not hunting and eating prey, then a natural diet is not wholly achievable in a home context.

THE CAT'S ANCESTRAL DIET

Cats are obligate carnivores, meaning that they must have some meat or animal tissue in their diet, although some specialist manufacturers have now prepared a 'vegan' diet for cats that overcomes this constraint. They are not omnivorous and scavenging, but fastidious and prone to food poisoning. Cats are able to catch and devour wild, living prey and the only vegetable matter they would naturally ingest is the bowel content of their herbivore prey, also consuming hair, skin, bone, cartilage, sinews and ingested matter, in addition to meat (muscle).

This ancestral diet may not be an attractive concept to humans and could result in damage to the local ecology, but it is instructive. It is logical to assume that, if we stray too far from this diet, our cats are likely to suffer ill health and poor development.

RAW MEAT AND BONES

In some households, the feeding of fresh fish or a recently killed pheasant, chicken or rabbit may be acceptable. If a cat is brought up on this type of diet from kittenhood, she will enjoy it. If not, some adult cats might reject this approach. Raw meat is better than cooked, but avoid pig meat as it appears to be less digestible to cats. Giving raw bones is also a possible option, but cats will usually only tackle small bones. Raw bones rarely splinter but the mineral benefits of bone can still be achieved by grinding raw bones thoroughly, if that offers a more acceptable lifestyle choice in some households.

OTHER DIETARY COMPONENTS

Cats require some vegetable material that needs to be in processed form, since they cannot chew it and in the wild their vegetation intake is partly digested. Vegetables can be puréed or blended, boiled or steamed. If using a juicer, feed the pulp (fibre) too. It is advisable to feed organically grown vegetables, carrots in particular, in order to minimize the potential risk of exposing your cat to chemicals in the diet.

Animal fat (raw), vegetable oils (not solvent-extracted), fish oils, cod liver oil and essential fatty acids (omega 3, 6 and 9) are all suitable supplements (see pages 20–21).

Water should be filtered or obtained from a spring or well. Softened water is usually unsafe. If buying water or when travelling, glass bottles are preferred over plastic.

Grain starch (see panel below) is not required, as it is not part of the diet of a wild cat, and in some cases it can be harmful.

Cows' milk and its products, such as butter, cheese and cream, especially if pasteurized, should be avoided wherever possible, as experience shows us that they are more likely to produce allergic reactions and digestive issues in cats. However, yogurt and cottage cheese may be acceptable, as a result of the process involved in their preparation. Experience also suggests that goats' milk and its products are well tolerated. Avoid salt and sugar, as well as chocolate, which can be toxic to cats.

FOOD AND WATER CONTAINERS

What type of receptacle you choose for your cat's food and water is an important consideration. Ceramic, china and terracotta or other pottery-type bowls, plates or dishes are recommended because they do not leach undesirable or toxic material into the diet. Enamelled metal bowls are acceptable, but plastic or stainless steel are not, since plastic

Pottery or ceramic bowls, dishes and plates are recommended to prevent contamination.

and its colorants are toxic and stainless steel may leach allergenic nickel and other metals into its contents. Cats prefer a shallow bowl with sloping sides or a plate because of the width of their whiskers. Feeding containers should be washed daily in very hot water.

ADVISED	NOT ADVISED
Raw meat	Pig products of any kind
Occasional raw bone	Grain starch, such as bread, toast, cake, pasta, rice, oats and wheat
Raw grated or puréed vegetables	
Boiled or steamed vegetables	Non-organic carrots
Boned cooked fish	Pasteurized milk and its products
Seaweed/kelp	Anything not fresh, especially meat
Organic eggs	Chocolate
	Salt and sugar
Ceramic or pottery bowls	Stainless steel or plastic bowls

SUPPLEMENTS

Supplements including minerals, vitamins, nutraceuticals and herbs can be added to your cat's basic diet in order to rectify a deficiency or fulfil a particular health purpose. Although some have their uses, such as brewer's yeast to deter fleas, most cats if fed a fresh, wholesome, natural and intelligently devised diet should need little in the way of supplements.

Herbal Echinacea can be added to a natural diet to aid immune function.

DIETARY IMPROVERS

If for any reason you consider that your cat's diet is lacking, omega 3, omega 6 and omega 9 fatty acids, brewer's yeast, bone meal or minced bone, seaweed (kelp), additive-free cod liver oil and linseed oil are excellent sources of additional oils, minerals and vitamins.

PRODUCTS FOR DISEASE SITUATIONS

Nutraceuticals may be recommended if your cat is suffering from chronic disease, for instance arthritis. Products that are often prescribed in such situations include methyl sulfonyl methane (MSM), usually derived from a by-product of the wood-pulping industry; chondroitin, usually from pig cartilage, bovine cartilage or shark cartilage; glucosamine, usually from the exoskeleton of crustaceans and green-lipped mussel (*Perna canaliculus*). However, these supplements should not be necessary if your cat's diet has been well devised in the first place and they can be quite expensive. It has also been quite difficult to prove the efficacy of these products; sometimes commercial needs can replace science in the marketing of nutraceutical and nutritional products.

If a cat is diagnosed with cancer, there is a wide range of products that offer possible benefits. Antioxidant and vitamin supplements, for example vitamins A, D, E and C, selenium and garlic, Echinacea and other herbs, co-enzyme Q10, capsicum, various patent teas, lycopene, enzymes and other supplements are available, and you

Minced black olives provide a natural source of iron in a diet.

Native American herbs, Ayurvedic herbs or Traditional Chinese Medicine (TCM) herbs. These products are usually formulated according to the general properties and virtues of the herbs they contain, and may be beneficial in a proportion of cats. However, it is advisable that herbs of whichever derivation should be formulated according to the needs of the specific individual feline patient in order to ensure a greater likelihood of benefit, and a vet skilled in the use of herbs should be consulted (see pages 44–45).

should research in print or online for guidance on their use. Unequivocal research supporting the efficacy of these products is not available and the debate surrounding complex supplementation continues. You should also bear in mind that each cat is an individual, so results will inevitably vary in any case.

In heart disease, vitamins E and B6, folic acid and antioxidants may often be recommended, but again there is conflicting evidence with regard to their value. You are advised to research the available information before deciding on a course of action.

If your cat is anaemic or has suffered blood loss, giving her a supplement rich in iron is a logical step. However, elemental iron can be unpalatable to cats and can cause nausea. As an alternative, consider giving your cat foods that are naturally rich in iron, such as liver, beetroot, black olives and red cabbage.

There are herbal supplements marketed for use in a variety of chronic disease situations that may consist of Western herbs,

A NOTE OF CAUTION

In general, supplements can be a force for imbalance just as easily as a force for balance in a cat's diet, and therefore you should exercise great caution in what you choose to use. The best insurance against chronic disease is to feed your cat a fresh, wholesome, species-suitable diet in the first instance (see pages 18–19).

Red cabbage is a natural source of dietary iron, which can aid recovery from anaemia.

PACKAGING AND LABELLING

When purchasing manufactured pet food for your cat, it is important always to read the small print on the label, which has to give certain information on its contents by law – being guided in your choice by the name of the product is not enough. Labelling laws differ from country to country, with no international standard.

PET FOOD LABELLING REGULATIONS

In the USA, pet food labelling is regulated at both the federal and state level. The federal regulations, enforced by the Center for Veterinary Medicine (CVM) of the Food and Drug Administration (FDA), establish standards applicable to all animal feeds: proper identification of the product, net quantity statement, manufacturer's address and a proper listing of ingredients. Some states also enforce their own labelling regulations. Many of these have adopted the model established by the Association of American Feed Control Officials (AAFCO). These regulations cover aspects of labelling such as the product name, the guaranteed chemical analysis, the nutritional adequacy statement, feeding directions and declaration of the food's calorific content.

WHAT THE LABEL TELLS YOU

The pet food product's ingredients are listed in descending order of inclusion rate. The term 'meat' has to refer only to striated muscle with or without the accompanying and overlying fat and the portions of the skin, sinew, nerve and blood vessels that normally accompany the flesh. If the label states 'meat meal', however, this can refer to a rendered product from mammalian tissues.

If a product is named 'rabbit for cats' or 'lamb for cats', it must contain at least 95 per cent rabbit or lamb in the pack. If two or more major ingredients are in the name, the combined inclusion of the named ingredients must be no less than 95 per cent.

If the ingredient name is qualified by another term, for example 'rabbit dinner for cats', then it must contain at least 25 per cent of that ingredient. Similarly, for two or more ingredients, the combined inclusion should be 25 per cent or more. The ingredients list will itemize all other ingredients, which you should check carefully, especially if your cat has a known allergy to a particular ingredient.

Manufactured foods are subject to strict but esoteric marketing regulations.

Minced parsley is an important source of nutrients and supports urinary health.

A manufacturer can only highlight another ingredient on the label, say a herb or cheese, if it makes up at least 3 per cent of the final formulation. If the food is labelled, for instance, 'rabbit flavour', the type must be the same size, style and colour for both words in order to avoid prominence.

The water content of a product is important and can affect its feeding value. For example, 'meat' contains about 75 per cent moisture, while 'meat meal' only about 25 per cent. A food can contain a maximum of 78 per cent moisture, unless it is labelled 'in gravy', 'in sauce' or 'stew'. The water content affects the proportions of other ingredients, whereby a product with more moisture may contain a higher proportion of protein than a drier food, despite a much lower declared percentage of protein.

Minor ingredients listed are often vitamins and minerals and may include artificial colours, stabilizers or preservatives.

Ethoxyquin is still permitted as an antioxidant in pet food.

If labelling implies that a food can be used on its own, such as 'complete' or 'balanced', then in the USA it must comply with the AAFCO Cat Food Nutrient Profile. The claims 'natural', gourmet' and 'premium' have no legally controlled status.

THE FRESH ALTERNATIVE

Regulations can only protect the consumer to a certain extent and it is impossible to legislate for every eventuality. You must also remember that each cat is an individual and your feline may not be suited to a particular manufacturer's product. Buying fresh food from a known source and preparing it at home is the only sure-fire protection against the pitfalls of the labelling system and feeding your cat fresh food is likely to be a healthier option than feeding processed food (see pages 26–31).

Carrots provide good nutrition but should be organically grown.

OBESITY AND WEIGHT CONTROL

It is clearly undesirable for your cat to be overweight or underweight. In general, it is fair to state that overweight results from excessive food intake and underweight from eating too little. However, there are other factors that can adversely impinge on your cat's body weight. In either case, it is advisable that you seek the advice of a vet.

Being overweight puts a strain on your cat's heart, limbs, back and other organ systems.

FOLLOWING THE WILD EXAMPLE

Obese animals are not seen in the wild. Emaciated or very thin animals are likewise not common in the wild, except in cases of disease or famine. This implies that fat or thin wild animals die quickly, are killed by their fellows or simply do not exist. The normal wild animal is well muscled and lean.

The logical conclusion is that a 'wild' lifestyle and diet are conducive to your cat having a healthy body. Conversely, domestication brings with it the possibility of unsuitable diets and incorrect exercise patterns, leading to unhealthy body condition. Experience has shown that cats fed a healthy, fresh diet, based on the natural wild diet, will usually maintain their body weight and condition almost automatically (see pages 18–19). In a domestic situation, you also have the opportunity to vary the quantity of food you offer your cat to moderate her weight if necessary.

Unsuitable diets can lead to obesity through excess of certain components at the expense of others. Furthermore, cravings can be induced by certain ingredients found in manufactured diets such as, possibly, salt and monosodium glutamate (MSG), leading to overeating. There is also the human element to take into account, where owners feel the need to feed their cats excessively or offer them extra titbits and scraps, thus exceeding a healthy intake of food each day. The Barbary apes on Gibraltar offer an interesting example of this human effect on animals, as those out on the Rock are slim, while those by the tourist shop are obese.

DEALING WITH WEIGHT PROBLEMS

If your cat is obese, in the absence of specific thyroid gland problems that can lead to overweight, it is advisable that you feed her a natural, fresh diet while seeking the advice of a holistic vet for a suitable feeding regimen. In particular, it would be wise to remove carbohydrate foods from the cat's diet altogether until a correct weight has been reached.

Cats with thyroid problems possibly induced by immune disturbance, often noticeable by laziness or overweight (underactive thyroid) or hyperactive, noisy and thin (underactive thyroid), should be taken to a vet for advice and care. Spaying or castration may also increase a cat's tendency to overweight.

If your cat is excessively thin, she should be checked by a vet for worms, thyroid excess, renal disease, malabsorption or other

Thinness or emaciation results from underfeeding, malnutrition or disease – consult a vet.

metabolic or endocrine problems (see pages 38–39, 62–63 and 84–85). Very old cats can lose muscle and body weight. In the absence of treatable disease, you should feed your underweight cat a natural fresh diet, with advice from a holistic vet on the feeding regimen and quantity of food. If your particular cat can tolerate animal fat in quantity, try feeding pieces of hard lamb or beef fat to help weight gain.

In addition, how much opportunity for exercise that your cat enjoys can affect her body weight and should be adjusted according to need. It is important to remember that, should your cat sustain an injury thereby restricting her mobility, her food must be reduced immediately to prevent her from becoming overweight.

DISEASE RATHER THAN DIET

Some diseases can lead to an impression of excess weight in a cat, whereas this may actually indicate a medical condition that requires intervention. Problems such as heart disease, leading to fluid accumulation in the abdomen, cancer with a swelling in the abdomen, pregnancy and Cushing's syndrome can all make a cat appear to be overweight when she is not.

NATURAL RECIPES

As we have seen, the argument for providing your cat with a diet as close to that of a wild cat is strong, but understandably some households may consider this too extreme. The following recipes offer a wholesome, modified natural diet, and many more ideas can be added to create a truly varied fresh feeding regime.

BASIC PRINCIPLES

These recipes may look different from those for human consumption. This is because they are not intended to make cat food look like human food, simply because your cat will not be looking for, or be able to appreciate, fancy food preparation. Most hungry cats prefer eating to aesthetics. However, the fresh ingredients can be sourced in the same way as your family's food and preparation methods may overlap. Although cooking is not part of a truly natural diet for a cat, it is acceptable, especially in the case of vegetable material (see pages 18–19).

Organic food is recommended, in order to minimize chemicals in your cat's diet. If your cat should fall ill, organic food becomes even more important. Supplements can be selected in order to compensate for any perceived weaknesses in the range of foods offered (see pages 20–21).

NUTRITIONAL BALANCE AND PORTIONS

Dietary balance cannot be achieved in every meal, but comes naturally from offering a variety of wholesome and species-suitable food over a period of time. The body is able to achieve dietary balance for itself. Offering only one type of food is likely to set up imbalances, for which the body cannot adequately compensate.

Portions should be judged according to the experience with your cat. A medium-sized cat would usually easily manage about 250 g (8 oz) fresh meat in a day, along with vegetables and oils.

SUITABLE VEGETABLES AND HERBS FOR CATS

Celery	Watercress	Thyme
Sweet potato	Various seaweeds (sea	Sage
Spinach	vegetables)	Fenugreek
Broccoli	Nettles	Garlic
Carrot (must be organic)	Parsley	Turmeric
Parsnip	Oregano	Coriander (cilantro)

RABBIT STEW

Note that raw wild rabbit may harbour tapeworm. The meat should be taken off the bone, since cooked bones are not recommended.

- Rabbit meat (wild), boned and cut into small chunks
- A little olive oil
- A few sprigs of parsley, rosemary, marjoram and thyme, finely chopped, or use dried rosemary and thyme or dried mixed herbs or herbes de Provence
- Vegetable stock (unsalted, so best home prepared) or water
- Sweet potato, carrot, celery, leek, turnip and onion, unpeeled and chopped
- Peas, shelled

Fry the rabbit chunks in the olive oil in a flameproof casserole for about 10 minutes. Sprinkle with the herbs.

Add the stock or water and bring to the boil. Cover with the lid and place in a medium-low oven until cooked through.

Add the chopped vegetables and peas and return to the oven for a further 45 minutes.

Give to your cat when cooled.

RABBIT PÂTÉ

This is a rich recipe, not one for the fat-intolerant cat.

- Rabbit meat, boned and cut into small chunks
- Beef or lamb suet
- Celery, parsley, coriander (cilantro), basil and watercress, finely chopped
- Carrot peelings
- Vegetable cooking water (unsalted), previously reserved

Put all the ingredients in a large saucepan and cover with the vegetable cooking water. Boil until tender.

When cooled, process in a blender or food processor until smooth.

Put into large ramekins to make daily portions and store in the refrigerator, where it will last for several days. If covering, avoid clingfilm.

VARIATION
Turkey, chicken, lamb, beef or liver could be used instead of rabbit.

SEA SURPRISE

Fish, such as mackerel, catfish, albacore, haddock, coley, monkfish (angler fish), sardines, halibut, whitebait, pollock, bream, whiting, cod, salmon (wild) (choose a species whose population is not threatened by overfishing and that has been fished ethically), seasoned with kelp powder and poached, steamed or baked

Dillisk mash

- A little margarine, sunflower oil or olive oil
- 4 g (¼ oz) dried flaked dillisk (dulse) seaweed
- 150 ml (5 fl oz or ¾ cup) oat milk or goats' milk
- 1 sweet potato, scrubbed and boiled until tender

Melt the margarine or heat the oil in a pan, add the dillisk and cook for 4–5 minutes.

Add the oat milk or goats' milk and bring to the boil.

Add the cooked sweet potato and mash well.

Serve the mash with the cooked fish, or any other dish, when cooled. The leftovers of mash will keep, covered and refrigerated, for another day.

ORGANIC LIVER CAKE

This is ideal for using as treats for your cat.

- 500 g (1 lb) organic lambs' or calves' liver
- 1 whole organic garlic bulb, peeled
- 1 teaspoon finely chopped fresh herbs, such as parsley, oregano, sage and/or thyme
- 175 g (6 oz) organic jumbo or porridge (rolled) oats

Put all the ingredients in a food processor or blender and process until thoroughly mixed. The mixture should be thick and heavy and not too wet. If too wet, add a few more oats.

Spread out into a greased baking tray (sheet) to a depth of about 5 mm (¼ in) and bake in a medium oven for about 15 minutes. It will be just crusty on the top, but pliable enough to break or cut into pieces easily.

Once cooled, cut or break into 1 cm (½ in) cubes. These can be frozen and defrosted as needed.

VARIATION

Dried herbs of your choice can be substituted for the fresh herbs.

WHOLESOME STEW

A nutritious meal that can be fed with the dumplings (see page 30).

- Beef or lamb meat, boned but left untrimmed of fat and gristle, cut into small chunks
- A little sunflower oil
- Carrots (must be organic), celery and broccoli, finely chopped
- Turnip, swede or parsnip, unpeeled and chopped
- A good sprinkling of kelp powder
- A few sprigs of parsley, finely chopped
- Vegetable stock (unsalted, so best home prepared) or water

Fry the beef or lamb chunks in the sunflower oil in a saucepan with a lid or flameproof casserole dish until browned all over.

Add all the remaining ingredients and bring to the boil, then cover with the lid and simmer on the hob (stove) or, if using a casserole dish, transfer to a medium-low oven and cook until very tender.

Give to your cat when cooled.

MEAT, HERB AND BONE SAUSAGE

This is suitable for a cat that may not be able to manage chunks of raw meat or whole bones. As this dish is uncooked, it shouldn't be kept for long, since cats can be prone to food poisoning.

- A portion of fresh lamb or beef, minced (ground)
- Half of that weight of fresh bone, finely minced (ground) (no splinters)
- A good sprinkling of kelp powder
- A good sprinkling of dried herbs (herbes de Provence or mixed herbs)

Simply mix all the ingredients together and give to your cat along with some mashed boiled fresh vegetables, moistened with olive oil.

TASTY AND NUTRITIOUS DUMPLINGS

Besides feeding to your cat on their own, the raw dumplings can also be added to a stew or casserole for the last 10 minutes of the cooking time.

- Shredded beef or lamb suet
- Gram flour
- Finely chopped or minced fresh herbs of your choice, according to season (parsley is excellent), or dried mixed herbs or herbes de Provence
- A good pinch of ground turmeric

Mix the suet with the gram flour – experiment with the proportions to achieve the desired texture. Then add the herbs and turmeric.

Mix in just sufficient water to make a workable dough, then form into separate balls of whatever size you wish (smaller ones will cook more quickly).

Cook the dumplings in a pan of boiling water for about 10 minutes.

VARIATION
Use vegetarian suet for a vegetarian version. If your cat is a curry lover, add a tiny pinch of ground cumin, coriander and cardamom for extra flavour.

EGG, MEAT, GOATS' CHEESE AND BEAN BAKE

This is a real 'protein fix' for yor cat.

- Beef, lamb, turkey, chicken, rabbit or pheasant meat, boned and cut into small chunks
- A little sunflower oil
- Broad (fava) beans, boiled until tender, or canned chickpeas, drained
- Soft goats' cheese
- Herbes de Provence
- Organic eggs

Fry the meat chunks in the sunflower oil until browned all over. Place in an ovenproof dish and mix with the drained boiled broad (fava) beans or canned chickpeas.

Crumble soft goats' cheese over the mix and sprinkle with the herbs.

Beat together as many eggs as you need to cover the mixture you have prepared and pour over.

Place in a medium oven and bake until set.

When cooled, cut off the required portion and offer to your cat. The remainder can be stored in the refrigerator for another day. If covering, avoid clingfilm.

BRAISED CHICKEN IN PEANUT BUTTER AND COCONUT OIL

This is another great 'protein fix'. If your cat is not fond of sauces, try the chicken on its own!

- Chicken meat, boned and cut into small chunks
- A little coconut oil
- Unsalted peanut butter or other nut butter
- Grated fresh parsley
- Ground turmeric
- Garlic, chopped

Fry the chicken chunks in the coconut oil until browned all over.

Add the nut butter, parsley, turmeric and garlic and cook. Cover and cook gently until the chicken is very tender.

Give to your cat when cooled.

VARIATION
Pheasant could be used instead of chicken, when available – fresh road-kill is fine, but beware of lead pellets if shot.

COTTAGE CHEESE OR GOATS' CHEESE SAVOURY DOLLOPS

For the cheese-addicted cat, for an occasional fix, but only as part of a rounded and varied diet.

- Cottage cheese or soft goats' cheese
- Gram flour
- Sesame flour
- Finely chopped or grated fresh herbs, such as chives, rosemary, garlic and/or parsley
- A little sunflower oil

Mix all the ingredients together thoroughly – experiment with the ratio of flours to cheese to achieve the right consistency.

Form the mixture into balls and then fry in the sunflower oil.

VARIATION
Use crushed cranberries or blueberries in place of herbs, for a special health-giving treat.

ROUTINE MEDICAL CARE
VACCINATION AND ALTERNATIVES

There are several serious infectious diseases that can kill your cat, including feline panleukopenia, feline leukaemia, feline infectious peritonitis, rabies and feline immunodeficiency virus. Some form of protection is essential, and there are vaccines for all these diseases but the latter. Nosodes offer a homeopathic option, and can be made for any infections disease.

Your cat may contract feline leukaemia from fighting or sharing dishes.

CORE VACCINATIONS

The normal 'core' kitten vaccinations consist of protective components against feline panleukopenia (enteritis), feline calicivirus and feline herpes. Feline leukaemia (leukosis) vaccination is becoming more routine. There is also a nosode (see page 34) available for each of these diseases, so ask your holistic vet for advice. Rabies vaccination is also a 'core' vaccination in the USA (see page 34) – compulsory by law in many states.

Feline panleukopenia (enteritis) is usually a fatal disease affecting all body systems, resulting in great suffering. The virus is very hardy and infectious. Thankfully, the disease has been rarely seen since the vaccine became widely used in kittens.

Feline calicivirus and herpes can be fatal in extreme cases, affected cats showing upper respiratory disease. Many cats survive, but can carry signs of chronic upper respiratory (congestion) or oral (gingivitis) disease, and may never regain full health. Vaccines are available, but have only proved to be partially effective.

Feline leukaemia (leukosis) (FeLV) is a potentially fatal viral disease. Spread is usually via saliva, so the disease can be transmitted when cats fight each other or when they share feeding dishes.

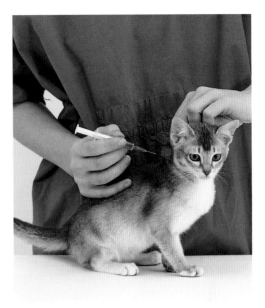

Vaccination is the conventional way to protect your kitten or cat.

'NON-CORE' PROTECTION

There are other diseases of cats, some non-fatal, for which vaccines are available. 'Non-core' vaccinations include protection against chlamydia, feline infectious peritonitis and ringworm.

Chlamydia is a bacterial disease spread by close contact only, and is usually characterized by conjunctivitis (see page 72).

Feline infectious peritonitis (FIP), once it has developed, is usually fatal. However, not all infected cats show signs and there is often a long delay between infection and disease. The name is derived from one form of expression of the disease, in which the abdomen becomes distended with fluid (the 'wet' form). The chest is also affected, but this is not visible, except via the respiratory distress it causes. There is also a 'dry' form,

in which no fluid accumulation occurs. Vaccination is available in the USA, but is relatively new and not necessarily effective.

Feline immunodeficiency virus (FIV) The disease, like human 'AIDS', occurs in a percentage of cats infected with FIV, and as with FIP, it rarely follows immediately upon infection. As is the case of human immunodeficiency virus (HIV), the illness may be from another unrelated disease that exploits the cat's reduced immune capability. Signs and symptoms of the disease are therefore extremely variable.

Ringworm is a fungal disease of the skin that usually responds very rapidly to homeopathic treatment, which also usually appears to be able to prevent its spread within the household. It can infect humans (zoonosis).

A wild animal can infect your cat with rabies via a bite.

THE RABIES THREAT

Humans can also be infected by rabies, making it a 'zoonosis' – a disease of animals transmissible to man. It is also potentially fatal in humans. The usual mode of spread is by a bite from an infected animal such as a bat, coyote, skunk, raccoon, wolf or fox. However, a domestic cat is considered more likely to infect humans and, for this reason, most states in the USA have laws that make rabies vaccination of cats compulsory. These laws may vary from county to county and from city to city, but cannot be less stringent than the respective state legislation.

The vaccination regimen that is specified by law can vary from state to state, usually from once every year to once every three years. The legal starting age can also vary

widely, and might be anything from eight weeks to six months.

While there is a homeopathic option, there is no alternative to legally-required vaccination shots. However, it may be that a kitten or cat can be given a 'nosode' and other homeopathic medicines by a holistic vet in an attempt to minimize any possible ill effects of the rabies shots (see pages 48–51).

HOMEOPATHIC PROTECTION

Nosodes are medicines prepared according to the same methodology as normal homeopathic medicines but they are derived from disease material, whether tissues, discharges or secretions. Because of the extreme dilution process (usually to the 30th centesimal dilution or 'potency'), no active material remains from the original infection, so they are safe and cannot cause infection (see pages 50–51).

Nosodes have been made from most infectious diseases of cats and new ones can be created to order by a pharmacy with the correct experience and equipment. Many cat owners in the USA and in other countries rely on protection by nosodes alone for the 'core' diseases mentioned on pages 32–33, with the exception of rabies, for which conventional vaccination is compulsory in most states.

THE VACCINATION DEBATE

There is a great deal of discussion about the necessity, advisability and safety of vaccination, as well as about the efficacy of nosodes. It is very difficult to obtain objective and impartial advice.

The internet will provide you with much to ponder in order to make an informed decision about which course of action to take. Certainly, there is no scientifically accepted proof of efficacy for nosodes as a means of protection against infectious diseases. Equally certainly, no manufacturer can claim 100 per cent safety for vaccine products and some opinions are that there are serious dangers in using them in cats. One particular vaccine is associated with tumours at the site of injection.

Vaccine products contain many more components than the required antigenic material. The list of possible 'other' ingredients includes mercury, aluminium, phenol, formaldehyde, antibiotics, oils, animal tissues and even the possibility of cancer DNA from continuous cell lines on which the viruses are cultured.

Science provides no definitive answer as to how often vaccine booster shots should be given. There is no scientific evidence to support an annual booster, and so the debate goes on, whether to revaccinate every second year, every third year, intermittently or once only.

Antibody titre testing gives only a very incomplete view of immunity. The presence of circulating antibodies indicates a level of immunity, but a negative result does not necessarily indicate lack of immunity. This test is often recommended to help decide whether revaccination is necessary, but it cannot serve as a complete guide.

There are many anecdotal reports of side effects of vaccination, with conditions such as skin disease, allergies, autoimmune disorders, tumours and cancer being cited, some including fatality. These far outnumber the officially reported cases. In a survey of cases conducted by the author, in those animals in which the start date of a chronic disease was certain, it was within three months of a vaccine event in 80 per cent of cases.

There are many cats in the USA and in other countries that are given nosodes as the sole means of protection and that have withstood definite local outbreaks and contact with the named diseases.

The protection of our precious pets against dangerous infectious disease is vital, therefore it is the duty of each owner to research the information available, whether in books or on the internet, to help when making a decision on how best to protect his or her cat. You may need to seek the advice of a holistic vet to help you to decide.

PARASITES – FLEAS

Fleas infamous for their irritating bite are a constant threat to your cat in the home, and they can bite humans too if they are hungry. Modern wisdom tends to recommend that you use powerful chemicals to control this threat, but there are more natural and ecologically friendly methods available to you.

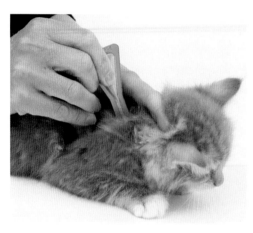

Modern conventional flea-killing compounds are often delivered by the spot-on method.

KNOW YOUR ENEMY

The cat flea, *Ctenocephalides felis*, is an insect parasite of cats with one pair of its legs being very powerful, allowing it to leap about 15 cm (6 in). An adult flea is about 2.5 mm (1/16 in) in length, and is narrow relative to its height. The flea feeds on a cat's blood but it breeds off the cat, in warm, sheltered, dark nooks and crannies. The larvae, which are about 4 mm (1/8 in) long, feed on dry blood and organic substances. In heavy infestations, the combination of greyish larvae and white eggs gives the 'nest' area a characteristic 'salt and pepper' appearance. Flea breeding is more active during the summer months, but heated houses can encourage year-round breeding. Other species of flea can also attack cats, and rabbits, hedgehogs or other wild animals can be a reservoir of infection.

HOW YOUR CAT IS AFFECTED

Your cat may scratch and groom excessively when she has fleas in her coat because of the irritant nature of their bites. Fleas can congregate on the head, neck, shoulders, sacrum (base of the tail) and tail head, but can feed anywhere on your cat. They can remain well hidden on cats with a long coat, but sometimes a flea can be seen scurrying across the less hairy part of a cat's abdomen.

Only in very severe infestations can a cat's vitality be threatened, but fleas can capitalize on a debilitated cat and may, even when as few as one or two fleas are present, set up allergic reactions and skin disease as a result of the nature of flea saliva. Fleas can also host part of the life cycle of tapeworms, which means that a cat with fleas may also harbour tapeworms (see pages 38–39).

FLEA-CONTROL OPTIONS

While a few fleas on a cat hardly represent a health threat, to humans or animals, neglect

NATURAL FLEA-CONTROL METHODS

Cat	House
Aromatherapy oils	Aromatherapy oils
Brewer's yeast	A piece of cedar or crushed chrysanthemum, fleabane or tagetes
Flea comb	Proprietary natural flea-control products
Proprietary natural flea-control products	Regular and thorough vacuum cleaning

of the problem can lead to serious infestation in the home as a consequence of the rapid reproductive cycle of the flea. Flea-control programmes must therefore be carried out on all cats and any dogs in the household as well as the home environment itself.

Diluted aromatherapy oils used on your cat can offer a very good first line of defence against fleas and an effective deterrent if the threat is not massive (see pages 52–53). Cedarwood, Eucalyptus, Garlic, Lemongrass, Lemon and Neem are well-known insect and flea repellents. These oils can be dropped into water and the diluted oils combed through the coat. Feeding your cat brewer's yeast can also act as a deterrent, since fleas do not like the flavour.

Combing a cat with a flea comb or using an electric flea comb can also be an effective method of control.

Chemical options are available from your vet for use in the home. More natural options are aromatherapy oils (see above), strategically placed around areas where a flea might choose to breed (carpet edges, skirting boards, floorboard cracks and down the sides of chairs). A piece of cedar, or crushed chrysanthemum, fleabane or tagetes may also act as a deterrent.

There are some proprietary products of natural origin on the market for flea control both for use on the cat and in the house. In the case of severe flea infestations, resort to strong manufactured chemicals may be necessary, but you can return to natural methods once the situation has been brought under control.

Aromatherapy oils can help the fight against fleas. Diluted oils can be combed through the cat's coat.

PARASITES – WORMS AND HEARTWORMS

Adult worms or their migrating larvae can damage the bowel, heart or lungs of a cat, depending on the species. Worm eggs can infect other cats and dogs, or can even be dangerous for humans, particularly children who may crawl on the floor or fail to wash their hands before putting them in their mouths.

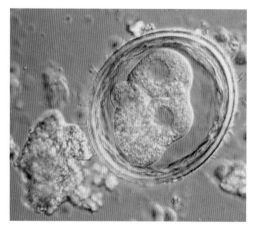

*Roundworms (*Toxocara cati*) commonly infect kittens via the mother's milk.*

ROUNDWORM (*TOXOCARA CATI, TOXASCARIS LEONINA*)

These worms inhabit the intestines, usually in kittens, causing a pot-bellied appearance, with a dry, scurfy coat. Loss of weight and condition are signs of this.

Kittens can be infected by toxocara via the mother's milk. All kittens should be assumed to be infected from birth, and your vet will advise on an appropriate de-worming programme. Adult cats can become infected by eating wild prey.

Unless your kitten or cat vomits an adult worm or passes one in faeces, clinical signs or microscopic examination of the stool for eggs are the only methods of detection.

It is not certain whether the larvae infect humans, but it is wise to keep your cat clear of roundworms in case. Regular laboratory examination of faeces is a sensible precaution, especially if you have babies or toddlers in the household.

HOOKWORM (*ANCYLOSTOMA* AND *UNCINARIA* SPP.)

Common parasites of the cat's intestines, these very slender worms are about 1 cm (½ in) long. Despite their small size, a large number of them can take a significant proportion of a cat's blood in a day.

Eggs from a cat's faeces settle on the ground and larvae hatch and survive on moist vegetation or earth. They can infect the cat by ingestion or via the skin. These worms may also infect humans.

TAPEWORM (*DIPYLIDIUM CANINUM*)

The tapeworm is a ribbon-like parasite of the intestines composed of segments that carry eggs, which break off and are passed via the anus. They can be seen with the naked eye, like moving grains of rice around the cat's anus or in the stool. The parasite can be a serious competitor for food and an affected cat can lose weight very rapidly.

Intermediate stages in the life cycle of the tapeworm are harboured by small prey animals, such as mice and wild rabbits. Fleas can also carry the infection, infecting a cat when eaten (see pages 36–37).

WHIPWORM (*TRICHURIS VULPIS*)

These are microscopic worms that inhabit the colon of cats, but rarely cause disease.

HEARTWORM (*DIROFILARIA IMMITIS*)

Heartworm occurs in the USA and the Mediterranean region but not in the UK. These worms can cause serious heart disease in cats if the infection goes untreated. They destroy heart muscle, resulting eventually in heart failure. Infection is via the bite of a mosquito.

STOMACH WORM (*OLLANULUS TRICUSPIS*)

This sporadic parasite inhabits the stomach of the cat and can cause stomach irritation and weight loss. It is acquired by a cat eating the vomit of an infected cat.

LUNGWORM (*ANGIOSTRONGYLUS* AND OTHER SPECIES)

The species of this parasite include *Capillaria aerophila*, *Aelurostrongylus abstrusus* and *Paragonimus kellicotti*. It is acquired by eating slugs or snails and affects the lungs, causing coughing, breathing problems and lung damage.

Tapeworms (Dipylidium caninum) *are picked up by cats through eating wild rabbits and other small creatures.*

HOW TO TREAT AND PREVENT

It is sensible to consult your vet about treatment and prevention of these various worm infestations. Conventional chemical de-wormers are generally very effective, if correctly chosen. Natural de-wormers are available on the market, but there is no published proof of their efficacy. Herbs that are well known for their reputed anthelmintic (destructive of worms) action include Wormwood, Wormseed, Lad's love, Southernwood, Santonin and Cat thyme (for roundworms) and Pomegranate and Male fern (for tapeworms). You are recommended to seek the opinion of your holistic vet if you wish to try natural de-wormers.

In the case of those parasites that have migratory stages within the cat's tissues, there is a chance that a nosode (see pages 34–35) could be made and may help to prevent or treat infestation. This is a poorly researched area, but your holistic vet should be willing to discuss options with you.

PARASITES – LICE, MITES AND TICKS

Lice, mites and ticks are ectoparasites of the cat's skin. Cats usually become infected through close contact with infected animals, except in the case of ticks. Lice and mites can cause your cat considerable irritation, with possible self-trauma, as well as hair loss, while blood-sucking ticks pose the real threat of spreading viral diseases. In serious infestations anaemia can ensue.

LICE

There are two types of louse that may infect your cat: *Felicola subrostrata* (the biting louse) and *Anoplura* spp. (the blood-sucking louse). Lice are insect parasites that are visible to the naked eye. However, they are very tiny and flattened dorso-ventrally, so seeing them can present a challenge, although a magnifying glass will help. If your cat is itchy, losing hair and her coat is in poor condition, a vet or cat groomer can help you to check for lice.

Lice spend their entire lives and life cycle on the cat, so infection is by direct contact with an infected cat. They lay their eggs (called 'nits') on the hair shafts, which may be

MITE CONDITION	SIGNS	MEANS OF INFECTION
Notoedres mange	An extremely itchy condition, causing hair loss and inflammation starting on the head at the base of the ears and spreading to the forehead and eyelids. It can spread to other parts, for example paws and hindquarters.	Usually by close contact with an infected cat.
Cheyletiella mange	Itchiness, especially along the back. Hair loss and dandruff are usually seen. Sometimes called 'walking dandruff', the mites can be seen with the naked eye or easily with a magnifying glass.	Usually by close contact with an infected rabbit or cat.
Ear mites	The mites feed on the lining of the ear canal and cause great irritation, leading to head shaking and scratching or rubbing the ears. A characteristic brown wax discharge can usually be seen.	Usually by close contact with an infected dog or cat.

PARASITE	TREATMENT
Notoedric mange	This can prove very difficult to clear, so sometimes the best treatment is a combination of aromatherapy oils, homeopathic Sulphur and chemical treatments
Lice and cheyletiella	These are usually easy to eliminate using either: Aromatherapy – regular application of Tea Tree or Neem oil. Chemical agents supplied by your vet
Ear mites	These can also be controlled quite simply using either: Aromatherapy such as Tea Tree or Neem oil, Iodoform powder or chemical agents supplied by your vet

In all cases, you are recommended to seek the advice of a vet or holistic vet.

visible. The life cycle takes about 21 days to complete.

MITES

Three types of mite can affect your cat: *Notoedres cati* (the face mange mite), *Cheyletiella* (rabbit fur mite) and *Otodectes cyanotis* (the ear mite) – see the panel left.

TICKS (*IXODES* SPP.)

These blood-sucking parasites spend most of the year in rough herbage, jumping onto a warm-blooded animal as it passes during the feeding season. Some ticks feed in the spring and some in the autumn.

Ticks are tiny when first attached to the skin, but grow as they fill with the cat's blood. They attach by burying their mouthparts into the cat's skin, making removal a skilled job if the cat does not do it. If a tick is incorrectly removed, a stubborn lesion can develop at the site of attachment.

Ticks are significant in that they can spread viral diseases, most notably Lyme disease.

HOW TO TREAT AND CONTROL

Regular grooming (see pages 16–17) provides a very useful opportunity for close inspection of your cat's skin and coat. It is usually enjoyable for your cat and it helps to promote a healthy coat and the control of external parasites. Combing and brushing will clear away any debris and can also remove lice or fleas or their eggs.

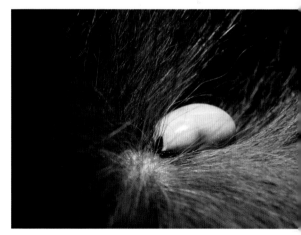

Ticks feed once a year, waiting in rough vegetation for passing mammals.

CASTRATION AND SPAYING

Female cats (queens) can produce a prodigious number of kittens in a lifetime, and adult male cats (toms) can become undomesticated. When deciding whether to neuter your cat or not, your pet's welfare with regard to the surgical procedures involved needs to be considered, as well as the social and welfare aspects of leaving cats to breed freely.

Courting and mating behaviour can be very noisy and anti-social in a residential area.

THE CASE FOR AND AGAINST

It is commonly recommended by welfare societies and communities in general that both male and female cats should be neutered. The author is against unnecessary mutilation of animals, but is persuaded, in the case of cats, that it is a necessity if they are to continue to be domesticated and if they are not intentionally being kept for breeding purposes.

While surgical removal of the ovaries and womb of a female cat and the testes of a male cat are undoubtedly mutilations, there appear to be remarkably few negative repercussions. Apart from the standard risks attaching to anaesthesia and surgery, the operations appear to be very routine and safe.

LIFESTYLE OF A QUEEN

If a female cat is not spayed, she will begin 'calling' at about four to six months of age (see pages 9 and 78–79). She is then able to become pregnant and have kittens. If she does not mate, the 'calling' can persist for two weeks or more at a stretch and can repeat every three weeks, during the months of February to November in the northern hemisphere. When 'calling', she will persistently yowl and roll over, squirming and rubbing.

If a female cat is mated, pregnancy lasts about nine weeks and she can give birth to up to ten or, rarely, even more kittens. Each year, this can represent a massive load on rescue and re-homing charities, and the season's influx of kittens usually decreases the chances of re-homing adult inmates.

LIFESTYLE OF A TOM

If a male cat is left entire, he starts to develop male body features (sexual dimorphism) after about six months of age. An entire male is usually larger than a castrated male and he develops bushier hair around the head region. He will become aggressively territorial and will actively seek a mate, sometimes ranging over a large territory. He will become increasingly less home oriented and will be involved in fighting on a daily basis. Of course, this results in injuries to other cats in the neighbourhood, apart from those he sustains himself. He also marks territory with urine, which acquires a strong and characteristic odour, not unlike that of a box hedge. Neighbours' houses, gardens and premises can become battlegrounds.

WHAT HAPPENS IN SURGERY

Neutering operations, whether spaying (ovarohysterectomy) or castration (orchidectomy or orchiectomy), are usually performed before the cat has reached six months of age. In this way, the male will not yet have taken on the morphological characteristics of a full tom and the female is not permitted to give birth to an unwanted litter of kittens.

In the case of a male, the surgery is relatively simple and quick, and does not involve cutting through the body wall. In the case of a female, surgery requires the opening of the abdominal cavity, either through the flank or through the ventral midline, in order to locate and to remove the ovaries and womb. This is major surgery, but appears to be taken as relatively minor by the vast majority of female cats.

RECOVERY AND AFTER-EFFECTS

Post-surgical recovery is usually rapid in both sexes, but it is recommended to administer homeopathic Arnica before, during and after surgery, in order to minimize trauma and pain and to speed healing. If there is obvious pain after surgery, homeopathic Hypericum can help. If there appears to be a general ill-effect from the surgery, whether physical or mental, homeopathic Staphisagria can help many cases. Should there be difficulty in recovering from the general anaesthetic, homeopathic Nux vomica will usually help. If there is post-surgical shock, homeopathic Aconitum may help.

If your cat does develop ill effects of surgery in the longer term, outside the immediate recovery period, these can arise from the act of removal of an integral part of the endocrine system (the ovaries), resulting in a hormone imbalance and disruption of the normal humoral control of the body and its functions. Affected cats (male or female) may be more likley to develop skin problems, such as over-grooming, alopecia and miliary dermatitis (see pages 66–67). This type of problem is not uncommon in veterinary clinics. More unusually, some male and female cats can tend towards obesity, possibly as a direct result of the surgery and the removal of the testes or ovaries.

RESPONSIBLE OWNERSHIP

The keeping of pet cats puts us in a position of responsibility and, although submitting your cat for surgery involves a type of mutilation, we cannot encourage indiscriminate multiplication of the cat population.

castration and spaying **43**

NATURAL THERAPIES AND TREATMENTS
HERBS

Although herbal medicine is the oldest medical practice known to man, it is the direct ancestor of modern Western medicine, and many modern drugs have derived more or less closely from plants. The Native North American culture was not a written one, but texts exist from ancient civilizations in China, Egypt, Greece, the Arab world and medieval Europe that include the medicinal use of herbs.

Elecampane is traditionally used as an anti-bronchitic and as an alterative.

A UNIVERSAL PRACTICE

All human cultures appear to have an active herbal tradition with a deep understanding of the value of herbs in maintaining health and treating injury and disease. There is evidence that animals use plants for medical reasons (zoopharmacognosy) and therefore herbal lore may be partly instinctive, even in humans.

HOW HERBS WORK

In herbal medicine it is not always possible to distinguish between the nutritional benefits of a plant and its medicinal properties. Whether for humans or for animals, there should never be a separation of medicine and nutrition and in herbal medicine the boundary is especially blurred.

Plants contain different classes of medically active substances, in unique combinations, including alkaloids, glycosides, saponins and flavones, which can provide one basis for their classification. Herbs can also be grouped according to their action, for example: anti-inflammatory, diuretic, expectorant, laxative/aperient, purgative, sedative, stimulant and tonic – see panel opposite. The skilled herbalist, whether practising Western herbal medicine, Traditional Chinese Medicine (TCM), Ayurvedic medicine or another herbal tradition, will choose individual herbs or a combination, to obtain the precise effects required for the patient.

HOW TO GIVE YOUR CAT HERBS

You can give your cat herbs as capsules, tablets, dry powder, 'tea' or fresh when in season, but not as an alcoholic tincture. Some herbs are not very palatable to cats, so you may need to disguise them in food (see pages 18–25). They act by exerting a direct medical or nutritional effect on the body and its processes.

It is vital in herbal medicine that plants should be identified correctly. They should be correctly harvested from unpolluted areas and, if cultivated, be grown without the use of modern agrochemicals. It is also advised that indigenous species should be used because they may prove more suited to the cat's constitution than exotic herbs.

A trend in modern herbal medicine is to identify a supposed 'active' ingredient, extract and purify it and use it in isolation. This is not holistic medicine and carries inherent dangers that are not involved when using whole plants. Ingredients of the whole plant tend to act in synergy and to balance each other in nature, whereas man disturbs this holistic balance with his 'interference'. Many products are now being marketed in this way, and it is then but a small step to the alteration of these supposed active molecules and the marketing of modern patent drugs. Adverse side effects are an accepted part of modern medicine.

COMMON HERBS AND THEIR ACTIONS

Herb	Selected actions
Angelica	Febrifuge – helps reduce fever
Black cohosh	Antispasmodic – relaxes muscle
Burdock	Alterative – produces a general healing tendency
Comfrey	Demulcent – coats and soothes mucous membranes
Dandelion	Diuretic – promotes urine flow
Elder	Diaphoretic – promotes sweat
Elecampane	Tonic – generally 'strengthens' the body
Flax seed	Aperient – promotes defecation
Garlic	Anthelmintic – discourages internal worms
Golden rod	Astringent – drying action
Hawthorn	Cardiac – acts on the heart
Hops	Nervine – healing benefit on the nervous system
Horseradish	Stimulant – boosts metabolism and excites nerve pathways
Marigold	Vulnerary – helps wound and injury healing
Pokeroot	Alterative – stimulates a general healing tendency
Sage	Carminative – prevents or eases abdominal flatulence
Skullcap	Sedative – calming agent
Tansy	Bitter – bitter taste, stimulates receptors in the tongue
Vervain	Expectorant – loosens mucus in the trachea

ACUPUNCTURE

Acupuncture is part of Traditional Chinese Medicine (TCM) and, if practised in a traditional way using manipulation, diet, lifestyle adjustment and internal medicine, is a deeply holistic form of therapy. Besides its role in veterinary medicine, it is also used as first-line medicine by a large proportion of the human population of the world.

PRESENT-DAY PRACTICE

Although acupuncture is part of Traditional Chinese Medicine (TCM), there are many modern adaptations that have been made in the light of experience and the needs of contemporary life. It is used in both man and animals, with cats being no exception.

Because of its highly specialized and complex application, it is recommended that acupuncture should only be carried out by a vet with appropriate experience and expertise. In some countries its use in animals is legally restricted to veterinary application, to protect animal welfare.

HOW IT WORKS

Typically, acupuncture consists of using needles to stimulate certain points in the body in order to balance energy flow and quality. However, stimulation of these points may also be performed electrically (electro-acupuncture) or by LASER (light amplification by stimulated emission of radiation), massage (acupressure), injection, implant and magnets.

TCM, which is around four thousand years old, teaches that the body energy (called 'qi', pronounced 'chi') flows rhythmically around the body through meridians or channels in a 24-hour rhythm. There are 12 meridians on each side of the body with the qi flowing in each for about two hours, thus giving the 24-hour rhythm. Modern science has now confirmed what is called the 'circadian rhythm', thus lending support to this model.

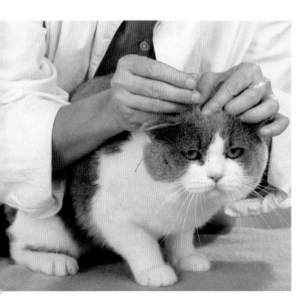

Cats accept acupuncture with equanimity or they appear really to enjoy it – relaxation is very common.

Ginger root is used in Traditional Chinese Medicine to correct coldness

failures than the use of the fully holistic application of the whole herb.

While this model of life, health and disease is very different from that of modern Western medical science, using acupuncture according to this model is able to produce effective results in many troublesome conditions.

HOW IT CAN HELP YOUR CAT

Acupuncture is most frequently used in cats for the treatment of locomotor problems such as back problems, neck problems, lameness, paralysis and arthritis (see pages 68–71). It is also employed as a means of pain control. Those vets most experienced in this form of therapy will also use it to tackle such conditions as liver problems, digestive problems, uveitis, epilepsy and other chronic diseases (see pages 64–65, 73 and 76–77).

Acupuncture cannot argue with conventional medication and makes a useful extra 'string' to the medical 'bow'. Many modern veterinary clinics have a veterinarian who is versed in the use of acupuncture and/or Traditional Chinese Medicine and can offer both acupuncture and conventional medicine. Please note that the author does not support the use of animal parts or endangered plants in TCM.

TCM also proposes the theory of yin and yang, the eternal opposites of which qi and every dynamic system is composed, and it is held that health depends upon the proper balance of yin and yang.

Imbalance between yin and yang or the disruption of the rhythm or flow gives rise to disease, and needling (or other means of point stimulation) is used to restore the balance. However, in the truly holistic practice of TCM, spinal manipulation, internal medicine (usually Chinese herbs, but may also be Western herbs or homeopathy), diet and lifestyle regulation are also used in support of needling (see pages 18–19, 44–45, 48–51 and 56–57). In modern Western countries, we tend to use needling alone in order to try and achieve the medical benefit of acupuncture. The author believes that this rationale is incomplete and will result in more

> ### CONDITIONS MOST HELPED BY ACUPUNCTURE
> Really strong indications are: arthritis, back problems, neck problems, injury, paralysis, megacolon and chronic sinusitis.

HOMEOPATHY

Homeopathy is medicine practised according to the 'Law of Similars', a natural phenomenon discovered formally by Dr Samuel Hahnemann in Saxony during the late 18th century. The practice has continued to this day, using principles derived from Hahnemann's extensive and meticulous writings, but with modern developments of the science.

Arnica montana – *used for the treatment of any injury or trauma.*

Law of Similars, that is any substance that can provoke symptoms or signs in a healthy body can be used to stimulate cure of disease displaying similar signs or symptoms.

Medicines are selected, not according to their pharmaceutical properties, but according to the symptom picture that the substance can provoke in a healthy body. They are extremely dilute, so cannot cause adverse or toxic effects, enabling the use of many otherwise toxic substances. The dilutions are often so extreme as to reach sub-molecular levels, giving rise to some of the criticism of the method by the scientific community. The misunderstanding occurs because modern medical science tends to think in terms of pharmacological action of a medicine rather than biological stimulus and response.

THE BASIC PRINCIPLES

Hahnemann lectured in Leipzig around 1813 on the use of homeopathy in animals, and this practice has been extensively developed and put to practical use ever since, in farm animals, horses and domestic pets.

Homeopathic medicines are derived from plant, mineral and animal sources, diluted to extreme levels and applied according to the

HOW IT WORKS IN PRACTICE

Homeopathic medicines can be used in a simple and effective first-aid context or they can be used in serious acute or chronic disease. However, the deeper or more serious the disease, the greater the skill and understanding required. Many medicines are available over the counter for domestic use, but for any serious disease, veterinary advice should be sought. An expanding number of vets have been trained in the use of homeopathy.

Homeopathic medicines can be given as tablets, powders or aqueous solutions, but not as an alcoholic tincture. They are usually acceptable to cats and can be placed in the mouth rather than having to be forced down the throat. Many cats will readily take them from a saucer or dropper.

Homeopathy treats the animal as an 'energetic whole', not as a collection of symptoms or signs with a specific disease name. Because we are treating the patient, not the symptoms, we need to know a great deal of information about the patient and its medical history, its background and its home environment. When you visit a vet, you therefore need to answer questions that can appear to be quite unrelated to the presenting problem. The holistic vet must then identify and remove those factors in the life of the patient that may impede healing, in order to maximize chances of a cure.

PREVENTATIVE HOMEOPATHY

One specialized area of homeopathic medicine is the prevention of infective disease by the use of nosodes (see pages 34–35). These are medicines made from disease material, usually to a 30c potency, and used for the prevention of specific diseases – a little like the principle of vaccination but without the risks. This method is currently without accepted proof of efficacy and should only be used under the expert guidance of an experienced holistic vet.

HOMEOPATHIC MEDICINES

The potentization process is the method by which a material is serially diluted and succussed (shaken by powerful strikes) to produce an 'energy medicine' for homeopathic medicines (also Tissue Salts – see page 55). Typically, a 'mother tincture' is prepared and one drop is added to nine drops (decimal scale, written 'd' or 'x') or 99 drops (centesimal scale, written 'c' or 'CH') of alcohol/water solvent and succussed. This process is repeated until the desired dilution or 'potency' has been reached, for example 30c, d6. Homeopathic pharmacists scrupulously prepare the medicines, with careful recoding of batches.

Some of the most commonly used homeopathic medicines in home prescribing are described here in outline detail, but you should seek veterinary guidance if in doubt.

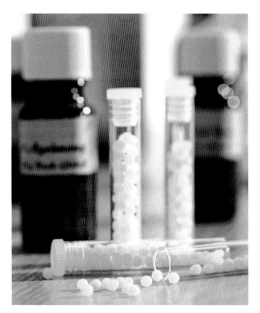

Many homeopathic medicines are available over the counter and are safe on account of their dilution.

Remedy	Used for
Aconitum napellus	It helps to restore balance after sudden disruption of equilibrium, whether fever, haemorrhage, fright, shock or injury. Acute inflammatory reactions, shock, chilling, overheating or sudden profuse haemorrhage all suggest this remedy.
Apis mellifica	Apis is indicated for shiny oedematous swellings, that retain the impression when indented, for example abscesses, arthritis with puffy joints and urticaria. It may help dysuria (difficulty in passing urine) if there is no actual obstruction.
Arnica montana	This is a medicine to be kept in every household. It is the first remedy for any case of injury, shock or surgery, and has a powerful action in combating sepsis of wounds, whether surgical or accidental.
Belladonna	This is a medicine suiting violent and sudden conditions, for example fever, abscessation, inflammation, convulsions and violent temper. Symptoms are worse for noise, touch or jarring and better for warmth and quiet darkness. A characteristic 'pointer' is a dilated pupil.
Calendula officinalis	This is used mainly as a topical lotion or cream, speeding healing of abrasions, reducing suppuration and aiding first-intention healing of wounds. It acts as a healing stimulus and is strongly 'antiseptic' in its action.
Cantharis vesicatoria	This may suit a cat showing a frequent urge to urinate, with an empty bladder (beware of straining with a full bladder, which may indicate obstruction). Inappropriate urination behaviour may also be helped.
Carbo vegetabilis	Carbo veg. is especially used in collapse or near-collapse, with a cold body and warm head.
Euphrasia officinalis	Euphrasia, as its folk name (eyebright) suggests, is an eye remedy, helping many cases of conjunctivitis or ulceration. It is used internally or in the form of eye drops.
Hepar sulphuris	This is used in cases of suppuration (pus formation). It is useful either as a preventive or curative treatment in septic injury, such as cat-bite cellulitis.

Remedy	Used for
Hypericum perforatum	Hypericum is used in cases of injury to extremities, where nerve endings abound, particularly toe or tail injuries. Post-operative pain, spinal injury, lacerated wounds and puncture wounds may be helped by this remedy.
Ledum palustre	Ledum is the first-choice remedy for puncture wounds. It also has uses in arthritic pain of the small joints that are cold to the touch yet worse for heat or warmth.
Natrum muriaticum	Sneezing, fluent coryza (mucoid discharge from the nose and mouth) with thin nasal discharge and watery eyes are typical indications. Deep grief can respond. Ill cats might seek solace in their own company and tend to appear sad, miserable and withdrawn.
Rhus toxicodendron	Rhus can be used if your cat's skin shows small red papules (pimples) or vesicles (little blisters) that are very itchy. Rheumatic symptoms are its greatest sphere of use, suiting signs that are worse for cold, wet conditions and for initial movement after rest.
Ruta graveolens	Ruta is homeopathy's sprain and dislocation remedy. It suits tendon, ligament, joint or bone injury.
Sarsaparilla	Its use in obstructive urinary problems in cats merits its place on the shelf. It can help a marginal case to resolve without surgical intervention. Itching sores on the head, especially occurring in springtime, are also characteristic.
Secale cornutum	This remedy aids circulation to any extremities, whether following injury or physiological change. It has been used to treat iliac thrombosis.
Silicea	Chronic inflammatory conditions and foreign body injury indicate Silicea. Examples are chronic sinusitis, thorn or splinter injury and chronic abscess.
Staphisagria	This is suitable for resentment and conditions arising from that emotion. It can be used to help post-operative problems and may also help inappropriate urination.
Symphytum officinale	This has an unsurpassed reputation for the speeding and regulation of bone healing.

AROMATHERAPY

The use of 'essential oils' derived from different plants is described as aromatherapy, although not all these medicinal agents are actually oils. The process by which these medicines are derived is distillation, which means that they include all the aromatic and volatile compounds of plants rather than just the oils.

The medicines are supplied in small bottles, since doses or quantities used are minimal.

THE BASIC PRINCIPLES

Since the medicines used in aromatherapy are derived from plants, there is a relationship to herbal medicine (see pages 44–45), but it is a highly specialized branch and the medicines can be extremely powerful. A very little can achieve much, so it is strongly advised that the general use of aromatherapy in animals is confined to expert vets. However, some aromatherapy medicines lend themselves to home use.

The route of absorption of these medicines is via the olfactory receptors, thus achieving very rapid transfer to the brain and bloodstream and distribution around the body as a whole. Cats are generally very sensitive to aromatherapy and willing to accept it, and of course their cooperation is encouraged because it is not forced into their mouths. Aromatherapy is, however, rarely used in cats for fear of extreme sensitivity, but the author has not encountered any problems with its judicious and moderate use.

HOW AROMATHERAPY IS USED

Medicines can be administered by steam inhalation, with the cat in a basket next to a bowl of steaming water, into which a few drops of the medicine have been placed. A towel can be placed over basket and bowl, to maintain the vapour near the cat. Alternatively, oils can be burned in specialist oil burners (care should be taken to ensure burners are safe) or in candles, or neat oils can be sprinkled in the room. Oils can also be applied to furniture or to bedding. An open bottle may even be held near the cat's nose – olfaction is a rapid and effective route of medication and one that has been exploited by many ancient civilizations.

HOW IT CAN HELP YOUR CAT

As in herbal medicine, the capabilities of aromatherapy medicines extend to deep and serious medical use for a wide range of chronic and acute illnesses in cats. However, home users are not recommended to attempt to deal with serious illness.

Aromatherapy compounds also have the ability to deter insects such as fleas and lice (see pages 36–37 and 40–41). Tea tree, Neem, Garlic, Lemongrass, Lemon, Eucalyptus, Cedar and Pennyroyal are known insect repellents (the latter is an abortifacient, reinforcing the message that uneducated use of aromatherapy can bring dangers). Except Pennyroyal, a few drops of the above oils can be dripped into water in a bowl and the water combed through your cat's coat, varying the mixture of oils from day to day. Unfortunately, this measure is of little use in protecting against ticks.

Lavender is a commonly used relaxant and calmative – cats respond very well to its calming properties.

COMMON AROMATHERAPY MEDICINES

Remedy	Action
Basil	Digestive
Bergamot	Analgesic – eases pain
Camphor	Stimulant
Chamomile	Nervine – relaxes and eases anxiety
Clove	Anaesthetic – useful for painful or itchy lesions
Eucalyptus	Expectorant and decongestant
Fennel	Galactagogue – stimulates a mother cat's milk
Garlic	Disinfectant – useful internally or externally
Lavender	Calmative – eases fears and anxiety
Myrrh	Astringent – aids oral hygiene and health
Peppermint	Carminative – helps in cases of flatulent colic
Rosemary	Stimulant and disinfectant – also useful for floor or surface cleaning
Tea tree	Disinfectant and insect repellent

BACH FLOWERS AND TISSUE SALTS

Bach Flowers is the name given to 38 remedies developed by late 19th-century-born homeopathic physician Edward Bach as medicines that would access disease via its emotional roots. Previously, in 1880, William Schuessler published his system of 12 Biochemic Tissue Salts, which he asserted were all that was required to restore health, since any imbalance of them in the body's cells would result in disease.

Bach Flowers and other flower essences stimulate healing of disease where emotions are involved.

HOW BACH FLOWERS WORK

Although collectively called Bach Flowers, Edward Bach's (1886–1936) remedies are confusingly not all, in fact, made from flowers. Since his pioneering development of this more intuitive approach to natural medicine, other flower essences have become widely used around the world, for example the Bush Essences from Australia.

For the most part, the medicines are made by first floating flowers in pure water, in direct sunlight, for three hours. Woodier parent material or flowers that appear in periods of

COMMON BACH FLOWER REMEDIES

Remedy	Emotions and demeanour
Agrimony	Stoical suffering, mental pain with calm demeanour
Cerato	Lacking confidence
Chicory	Possessiveness and jealousy
Impatiens	Impatience, hurried demeanour
Mimulus	Shyness, reserved nature
Rock rose	Terror
Vervain	Tense and anxious
Walnut	Sensitivity to change
Rescue remedy	A combination remedy given for shock, distress or panic

COMMON TISSUE SALT MEDICINES

Medicine	Used for
Calc. fluor.	Supports tissue elasticity in ligaments and blood vessels, and helps bones and teeth
Calc. sulph.	Its cleansing action helps to maintain a healthy skin and to treat furunculosis, papules (pimples) or acne
Ferrum phos.	Respiratory problems, blood health, sore throats and bleeding, and to help aged cats
Kali phos.	Cases of nervous tension and nervous exhaustion
Kali sulph.	Catarrh and skin ailments
Natrum mur.	Fluent coryza (mucoid discharge from the nose and mouth) and for loss of smell or taste
Silica	Aids structure of skin and nails, and used to reject purulent infection

reduced sunlight are prepared by boiling in water for 90 minutes. The resultant solutions are mixed with brandy to make the 'mother tinctures'. The medicines are gentle and effective, producing no side effects. They are readily accepted by cats, as they are well suited to the intuitive nature of animals in general because they are employed on the basis of the emotions, demeanour and mood of the patient, treating even organic disease via the mind and emotions. The only challenge is in determining the relevant mental state of the feline patient. Physical signs are not listed among the indications.

These remedies are fully compatible with homeopathic treatments (see pages 48–51), provided that they are properly integrated.

TISSUE SALTS AND THEIR BENEFITS

These medicines are prepared by the same serial dilution and succussion dilution method as homeopathic medicines, to a 6x (d6) potency (see page 49). They are usually obtained as friable soft tablets and are well accepted by cats.

The author has used these medicines, including a new range devised in the light of modern agriculture, diet and lifestyle developments, not only in the treatment of ailments and illnesses but also to help to correct deficiencies of minerals that have occurred through problems of assimilation.

Bach Flowers and other flower essences stimulate healing of disease where emotions are involved.

CHIROPRACTIC AND OSTEOPATHY

Incorrect spinal and skeletal alignment, with associated impaired joint and muscle function, is not only painful for your cat but results in compensatory changes in her posture and movement, which in turn can lead to further damage. Chiropractic and osteopathic manipulation therapies aim to correct alignment and function, thus relieving pain and restoring proper posture and movement.

CONSEQUENCES OF SKELETAL MISALIGNMENT

The skeletal system is composed of the axial skeleton (head, neck, thoracic spine, lumbar spine, sacrum and tail) and the appendicular skeleton (the limbs). The pelvis operates as part of the axial system. The units of the skeleton (the bones) articulate with each other at joints, and muscles provide the motive power to operate the joints. Nerves emanate from the axial skeleton, to innervate the muscles. The correct integration of this system results in the fluid and pain-free

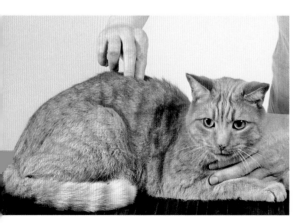

Chiropractic manipulation is a gentle means of restoring correct body function and alignment.

motion that we expect from a healthy cat. When there is misalignment or muscle spasm, pain and incorrect function ensue, with possible nerve involvement and further functional alteration. The body compensates for this by incorrect posture and movement, often resulting in further damage as a result of the abnormal load put on other parts of the musculoskeletal system. The prospect of a harmful spiral is then obvious.

HOW MANIPULATION THERAPY CAN HELP

Chiropractic and osteopathy are two branches of manipulative therapy that act in support of medical intervention. Within each practice there are widely differing techniques, so a general and complete definition of either technique is not possible. The effect of manipulative therapy is that, by gentle, judicious manipulation, muscle spasm can be relieved, joint alignment can be restored, nerve impingement released and posture and function corrected. This brings about reversal of the harmful spiral described.

Conditions in cats that are most clearly and directly helped by this intervention are neck pain, back pain, facial and cranial

BONES IN THE FELINE BODY

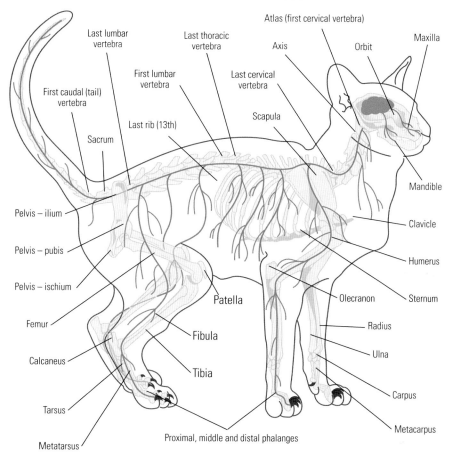

Atlas (first cervical vertebra)

Last lumbar vertebra

Last thoracic vertebra

Axis

Orbit

Maxilla

First lumbar vertebra

Last cervical vertebra

First caudal (tail) vertebra

Last rib (13th)

Scapula

Sacrum

Mandible

Pelvis – ilium

Clavicle

Pelvis – pubis

Humerus

Pelvis – ischium

Patella

Olecranon

Sternum

Femur

Radius

Fibula

Calcaneus

Ulna

Tibia

Tarsus

Carpus

Metatarsus

Proximal, middle and distal phalanges

Metacarpus

misalignment, pelvic misalignment and many cases of hind limb weakness or paralysis. However, a large percentage of feline patients, on routine examination, display back, neck and pelvic problems that have often gone undetected. Feline patients that have been successfully treated show obvious relief, which can be almost immediate.

AN INTEGRATED APPROACH
These manipulative therapies are not, however, stand-alone treatments, but operate in support of acupuncture, herbal medicine, homeopathy and conventional medication, depending upon the preference of the cat owner or vet (see pages 44–51). In many cases they add an essential extra dimension, without which success cannot be achieved. Depending upon how long the problem has persisted before treatment, muscle tone and strength and joint flexibility may also require the use of physiotherapy, to complete the restoration of normal and pain-free function (see pages 58–59).

chiropractic and osteopathy **57**

OTHER PHYSICAL THERAPIES

There is a wide choice of physical therapies, depending upon what suits the needs of your individual cat. Some of the best known are discussed here. These therapies act in support of medical input, such as herbal medicine, homeopathy, acupuncture or modern medicine and can be used in conjunction with chiropractic or osteopathic manipulation. Veterinary supervision is required.

A massage can be an enormously rewarding experience for both you and your cat.

PHYSIOTHERAPY

This is a non-specific umbrella term used to describe many forms of hands-on and exercise therapies that work to restore normal function and range of movement to the musculoskeletal system. It can also cover the use of instruments such as LASER (light amplification by stimulated emission of radiation), ultrasound, TENS (transcutaneous electrical nerve stimulation) and faradic stimulation. It is not a system of medicine in its own right, but should be used as an adjunct to medical input.

MAGNET THERAPY

This uses magnets applied to specific areas of the body in order to encourage circulation and to stimulate healing. Magnets are usually applied for limited periods of each day, rather than being used for 24 hours. Small magnets have been designed for applying with adhesive tape for localized action.

MASSAGE

A hands-on therapy that anyone can learn, massage can be quite strenuous for the masseur or masseuse at first, but becomes easier with practice. It is very rewarding, since a cat will clearly demonstrate where she enjoys or needs a massage and she will find a way to indicate whether more or less pressure is required and when sufficient massage has been received in one place or in a session.

Massage releases tension in muscles and allows the musculoskeletal system to operate in a more normal manner, with resulting benefits in posture and motion.

LASER THERAPY

This therapy uses cohesive light (usually infrared, but other colours can be employed for specialist purposes) to stimulate the healing of tissues such as muscle, tendons, ligaments, fascia, tendon sheaths and joint capsules. The probe contains a light-emitting diode that can be set to deliver the beam at different pulsed frequencies. Different probes are required for different wavelengths (colours).

LASER therapy differs from LASER surgery in that it uses a 'cold' LASER, which cannot destroy tissues. It it a very safe therapy, but the beam can damage the retina of the eye if accidentally aimed or reflected towards the pupil.

ULTRASOUND THERAPY

It is a therapy that employs the vibrations of ultra-high frequency sound beyond the range of human hearing, transmitted to areas of the cat's body by means of a probe or head. This creates a powerful and localized form of

LASER therapy stimulates the healing of skin, tendons, ligaments and muscles.

massage, and stimulates healing in soft tissues, such as muscles and tendons.

The cat's coat is usually shaved and a gel applied in order to achieve good contact with the skin. Care has to be exercised not to apply ultrasound over bone and not to any area for too long. It is advised that an appropriately skilled vet should be consulted.

TELLINGTON TOUCH

This is a method of improving balance and coordination through hands-on contact and exercises. It works on the principle that a cat can develop patterns of tension, which in turn can create stress elsewhere in the body and affect the cat's wellbeing and behaviour.

Signs of tension areas in a cat may include a local change in fur pattern, a patch of dry skin or exaggerated skin reflexes when touched.

COMMON AILMENTS
HEALTHCARE AND YOUR VET

While you are ultimately responsible for the health of your cat, advice and support from different sources can be essential to ensure that any health and management programme is the best that can be devised. Your vet is trained in the recognition of early signs of disease, knows the range of diseases and problems that can affect your cat's health and is in touch with the latest developments.

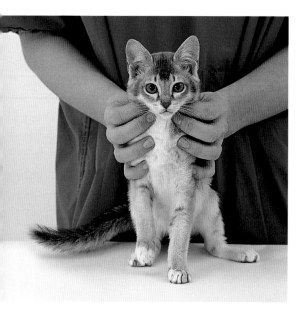

Your vet can recognize the early signs of disease, so an annual or six-monthly check-up is a good precaution.

ROUTINE HEALTH CHECKS

Regular veterinary checks for your cat are recommended to ensure that there are no signs of ill health and that your health programme is on course. These should be at least annually for younger cats and at least twice yearly in the case of older cats. If this check-up is with a holistic vet, he or she will be fully conversant with any holistic measures you have in place. If not, then some discussion and explanation will be necessary. If no holistic vet is available in your locality, you can arrange for a more distant holistic vet to communicate with your local vet. Even if a holistic vet is not involved, regular veterinary support is still advisable.

An annual blood test is also a good precaution, in support of a clinical examination. You may also consider it worthwhile regularly taking in urine and faeces samples in order to monitor your cat's health. If any sign of disease is found at a regular check-up, your vet may recommend investigations aimed at identifying a problem that may be present, so that a relevant treatment programme can be devised.

COOPERATION BETWEEN HEALTH ADVISORS

If your wish is for one or other form of holistic or natural veterinary treatment to be

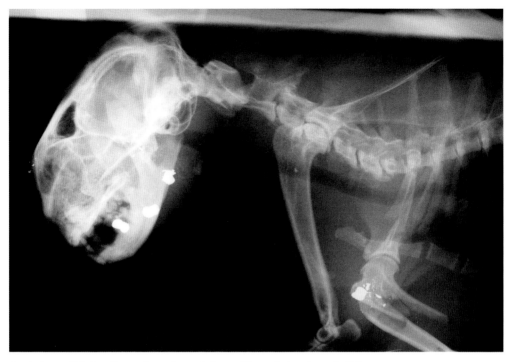

A veterinary clinic has diagnostic equipment along with surgical and care facilities.

employed and your local vet is not a holistic vet, you may need to travel farther for that help. However, it is still important to keep your local vet closely in touch with what treatments are being employed and with progress, so that any potential emergency response can be appropriate to the whole case. If more than one vet is working for your cat's health, it is vital that they are in communication and cooperating with each other, for your cat's welfare.

WORKING WITH YOUR VET

If you have the confidence or experience to carry out some home treatments, depending upon what is wrong with your cat, again it is advisable to keep your vet in touch with what you are doing and how things are progressing. It may even be that you can work with your vet, using your treatments and your vet's diagnostic and monitoring skills, to ensure progress.

Whatever arrangement is appropriate to your individual circumstances and your cat's special needs, it is never constructive for there to be arguments and conflict about the form of treatment being used. Maintain cooperation by keeping communication going and discussing any issues of concern in advance of problems arising. Your wish will be for your cat's optimum health and wellbeing at all times and your vet's motivation will be the same, thus ensuring that you work together for your cat's welfare, to ensure its most rapid and effective return to health and wellbeing.

FIRST-AID CONDITIONS

In emergency situations or when injury occurs, prompt action can make all the difference. You can safely give these homeopathic medicines to your cat while awaiting attention from your vet without fear of interfering with any other medical treatment – homeopathic and aromatherapy remedies can be given even to a collapsed cat, since the medicines do not need to be swallowed.

HOMEOPATHIC TREATMENTS

Problem	Remedy
Abrasions	Hypericum and Calendula lotion topically, Hyssop (aro).
Abscess	Hepar sulphuris (hom) if acute, Silicea (hom) if chronic, warm saline bathing.
Anaemia	Ferrum phosphoricum (t/s), Cinchona (hom) – give both and feed red/purple vegetables, black olives and liver.
Bites (cat or dog)	Collidal silver and/or Hypericum and Calendula lotion topically, Hepar sulphuris (hom), Arnica (hom) – give both, Hyssop (aro).
Bites (insect)	Hypericum and Calendula lotion topically, Aloe vera juice (herb) topically, Apis (hom).
Bites (snake)	Lachesis (hom) – the bushmaster, Vipera (hom) – the adder, Crotalus (hom) – the rattler. Professional advice may be needed to decide upon which to use.
Bleeding	Hamamelis (hom) – for dark oozing, Aconitum (hom) – for red gushing, Millefolium (hom) – for red seeping, Phosphorus (hom) – for bleeding tendency.
Bruise	Arnica (hom), Comfrey (herb) – both can be given topically and internally, Bergamot (aro).
Burns	Urtica (hom), Arnica (hom), Cantharis (hom) – give all three.
Catarrh	Natrum muriaticum (hom), Pulsatilla (hom), Eucalyptus (aro).
Collapse	Carbo vegetabilis (hom), Aconitum (hom) – give both, Camphor (aro), Rosemary (aro).
Convalescence	Cinchona (hom), Phosphoric acid (hom) – give both.
Crushing injury	Arnica (hom), Hypericum (hom) – give both.

LIST OF ABBREVIATIONS

hom homeopathic (see pages 48–51)
herb herbal (see pages 44–45)
t/s Tissue Salts (see page 55)
b/f Bach Flowers (see page 54)
aro aromatherapy (see pages 52–53)

Homeopathic medicines should be
given internally in 6c or 30c potency
(see page 49).

Problem	Remedy
Cuts	Hypericum and Calendula lotion topically, Staphisagria (hom).
Foreign body	Myristica (hom), Silicea (hom), poulticing, such as magnesium sulphate/glycerine paste, also known as Morison's paste.
Fractures	Arnica (hom), Symphytum (hom), Comfrey (herb), Boneset (herb) – all can be given concurrently.
Glands (swollen lymph nodes)	If generalized, this could be a general illness or a cancerous condition (see pages 86–87). If localized, it is probably the result of a local source of infection. Hepar sulphuris (hom) would be appropriate for the latter.
Hairball	Nux vomica (hom), a proprietary preparation containing milk of magnesia or liquid paraffin by mouth.
Haemorrhage	See Bleeding.
Heatstroke	Glonoinum (hom), Aconitum (hom) – give both.
Oil contamination	Petroleum (hom), Dandelion root and leaf (herb), vitamin C, plus consult a vet for decontamination.
Paralysis	Aconitum (hom) – pain and shock, Arnica (hom) – pain and healing, Hypericum (hom) – nerve damage and pain, Bergamot (aro) – pain. All may be useful and can be given concurrently; **spinal injury** Apis (hom) – spinal cord oedema, Nux vomica (hom) – spasm, pain and problems urinating or defecating; **iliac thrombosis** Lachesis (hom), Secale (hom). Acupuncture may be very helpful for any paralysis condition.
Poisonings	Nux vomica (hom), plus seek professional advice for the specific poison.
Post-operative recovery	Arnica (hom) – injury, Staphisagria (hom) – surgical injury, Hypericum (hom) – pain, Nux vomica (hom) – anaesthetic after-effects.

GASTROINTESTINAL PROBLEMS

Gastrointestinal problems are often observed by vomiting or by changes in faeces or defecation. They may also be noticed because of abdominal size, changes in appetite and weight loss in your cat. These signs can be transitory or may indicate deeper and more serious disease, so you are advised to seek veterinary help.

Cats eat grass, possibly to clean the stomach or in an attempt to clear worms.

ANAL GLANDS

If your cat's anal glands keep filling, homeopathic Silicea may help. It is also wise to take a look at your cat's diet – does it offer enough roughage (vegetable fibre)? Herbal Psyllium husks may help to bulk out the stool. The anal glands serve an excretory function and unsuitable dietary ingredients such as chemicals and toxins can cause problems. While not common in cats, this condition can cause distress.

APPETITE

A decreased or increased appetite may signal deeper health problems with your cat, so ask your vet for a check-up. Homeopathic Lycopodium or Nux vomica may help a poor appetite, while Calcarea phosphorica or Phosphorus may help pica (the eating of strange and unusual material, such as cloth, coal, wood or earth). Because pica can arise from diseases such as feline leukaemia (leukosis) and feline immunodeficiency virus, a vet should be consulted. Fabric chewing is quite commonly seen in Oriental breeds like the Siamese and it is normal for cats to eat small amounts of grass.

CONSTIPATION

If there is constipation, check with your vet for possible causes. Homeopathic Sulphur, Silicea, Nux vomica or Alumina may help. Herbal Psyllium husks in the food form a lubricating gel and bulk aperient (laxative). In the short term, herbal Senna can be helpful. Feed your cat plenty of vegetables. Megacolon arises from paralysis of the hindgut, some cases of which may be helped by combined acupuncture, chiropractic, homeopathy and aperient management.

DIARRHOEA

Your cat may experience acute diarrhoea as a necessary means of eliminating toxins acquired from unsuitable food, but consult your vet if the problem persists. If your cat is suffering from gastroenteritis, homeopathic Arsenicum (in the case of a dry mouth), Mercurius solubilis (with a wet mouth) or Mercurius corrosivus (with a wet mouth and dramatic straining) are often helpful.

HAIRBALL

Cats can accumulate hair in the stomach, during the process of grooming, which can lead to a cough or retching. Administering a proprietary preparation containing milk of magnesia or liquid paraffin can help them to bring it up. Homeopathic Nux vomica can be effective in stubborn cases.

INCONTINENCE

If your cat involuntarily defecates in the home, where it is lying or on the move, this is a case of faecal incontinence, which may indicate a veterinary problem. If it happens as a consequence of old age, homeopathic Causticum may help. Inappropriate defecation, on the other hand, can be behavioural in nature (see pages 80–81).

LIVER

There are many liver remedies available. Homeopathic Lycopodium (for flatulence), Nux vomica (for constipation), Chelidonium (for jaundice, especially obstructive), Phosphorus (for inflammatory conditions with jaundice) and Carduus (for a swollen liver) are possibly the most widely used. Herbal Milk thistle is a very well-known liver treatment.

Oral health is essential to general well being and health.

TEETH, GUMS AND BAD BREATH

Bad breath, gingivitis and dental scale are common in cats. These problems can arise from diet or immune damage, possibly by calicivirus or vaccination (see pages 32–35). Feeding chunky raw meat and fresh small bones to chew from kittenhood helps, although an older cat may not adapt to this (see pages 17–19). Applying Myrrh (as herbal tincture or diluted aromatherapy oil) can help gingivitis. Homeopathic Mercurius solubilis (profuse saliva) or Pyrogen (rotten odour) are helpful. You can remove tartar from your cat's teeth with a thumbnail or ask your vet.

VOMITING

This can be a sign of serious disease in your cat, so consult your vet. If gastroenteritis is diagnosed, Arsenicum (with a dry mouth), Mercurius solubilis (with a wet mouth and yellow frothy vomit) or Mercurius corrosivus (with a wet mouth and clear mucoid vomit) can put a rapid stop to the problem.

SKIN PROBLEMS

Skin disorders can be complex in cats and often betray underlying constitutional, hormonal or immune-mediated problems. If they result in a reduction in your cat's wellbeing, veterinary help is essential. Most homeopathic and herbal medicines have some action on the skin, which makes selection of the most appropriate and effective remedy a complicated process.

Excessive scratching can indicate ear or skin problems.

ACNE

Often occurring on the chin, acne is a sign of immune imbalance, permitting staphylococcal infection. Homeopathic Graphites or Sulphur may help, along with ensuring that your cat's diet and general health are optimal.

ALOPECIA

Loss of hair in your cat can signal deeper disease, so consult your vet. It may be the result of hormonal imbalance (see pages 78–79 and 84–85) or parasites. If there does not appear to be another cause, homeopathic Sepia or Arsenicum may be useful.

COAT SHEDDING/EXCESSIVE MOULTING

This may occur as a consequence of central heating or it may be of dietary or hormonal origin. See also Alopecia.

DANDRUFF/SCURF

Scurf may be due to general dietary or skin problems in your cat. To help prevent the problem, feed your cat omega 3, 6 and 9 oils (see pages 20–21). Homeopathic Arsenicum, Pulsatilla or Sulphur may be suitable, according to your cat's individual characterstics. *Cheyletiella* (rabbit fur mite) infestation may mimic dandruff (see pages 40–41).

ECZEMA

This is a loose term usually applied to skin disorders characterized by dry patches. Your cat may also have scabs or experience itchiness. Some useful medicines are homeopathic Sulphur if your cat likes cool conditions and the problem is exacerbated by warmth, Graphites if she likes warmth but is made worse by warmth and tends to be overweight and lazy, and Psorinum for a cat that likes and is improved by warmth. Zinc and castor oil cream or ointment may help to treat any sores but cats are notorious for licking off any topical treatments.

ITCHING/PRURITUS

If not due to fleas, lice or mange (see pages 36–43), excessive itching in your cat may be dietary or immune related (see pages 82–83), so seek veterinary advice. If the problem is allergic or constitutional in nature, homeopathic constitutional prescribing can usually help. Medicines commonly used in treatment are Agaricus, Calcarea carbonica, Graphites, Natrum muriaticum, Psorinum, Pulsatilla and Sulphur, prescribed according to the feline patient's individual constitutional characteristics and indicators.

MILIARY DERMATITIS (MILIARY ECZEMA)

This is a skin disease characterized by scattered tiny scabs and pustules that appear over the cat's body, usually accompanied by hair loss and inflammation, and is very itchy. There may be an autoimmune component to the disease (see pages 84–85). See Eczema (opposite) for treatment possibilities.

NAILS

Breaking, splitting or very soft nails are a sign of disease, which may be a local infection or part of a more general skin problem or autoimmunity (see pages 84–85). Sometimes the nail bed can become infected. Make sure that your cat's diet is adequate in zinc, sulphur and biotin. Homeopathic Silica or Graphites may be relevant in treating nail problems, especially if nails are crumbling or are brittle.

RINGWORM

This is a disease that is infectious to humans (a zoonosis) and is a fungal infection. It may or may not be itchy and your cat may not show any signs of the problem. Ultraviolet light is one of the tests that can be used to detect it and a laboratory can also examine a skin scraping. Ringworm is usually rapidly resolved by homeopathic treatment with Bacillinum, despite its reputation for being refractory to treatment.

RODENT ULCER

Despite its name, this problem has nothing to do with rats or mice and is possibly an autoimmune condition, in which the edge of the cat's lip is eroded and inflamed (see pages 84–85). The name comes from a similar-looking human disease. It is commonly treated with steroids or hormones in conventional practice, but homeopathy and LASER therapy usually clear it (see pages 48–51 and 59). Seek holistic veterinary help.

TUMOURS AND WARTS

Warts found on your cat may be helped by homeopathic Thuja, Calcarea carbonica, Lycopodium or Causticum. Herbally, a local application of the sap of Greater celandine, Dandelion or Caper spurge may remove the wart. For the treatment of tumours, see pages 86–87.

LOCOMOTOR PROBLEMS

Diet can have a very powerful influence on your cat's skeletal health in both the long and short term. It is important that you seek a chiropractic evaluation to ensure that your cat has the correct skeletal alignment, posture and optimal weight distribution. Massage and/or other physical therapy can be highly beneficial for your cat's musculature if it should be injured or in spasm (see pages 56–59).

Symphytum officinale, *known as 'knitbone', has a* *reputation for aiding the healing of bones.*

ARTHRITIS

This term literally means inflammation of a joint. Osteoarthritis is where there are bony changes around the joint. A simple sprain can also be referred to as arthritis (see opposite).

Rarely, septic (infected) arthritis can occur in cats. Common helpful homeopathic medicines are Rhus toxicodendron (if worse in cold and damp and stiff on rising but limbers up), Bryonia (if worse for any movement), Ruta (for sprains and strains), Rhododendron (if worse in thundery weather) and Calcarea fluorica (for osteoarthritis). Herbally, common medicines are Willow bark, Meadowsweet, Comfrey and Devil's claw. Acupuncture, Acupuncture-by-LASER and LASER therapy can also be helpful for arthritis, which is one of the most common fields of application of these therapies (see pages 46–47 and 58–59).

DEGENERATIVE JOINT DISEASE (DJD)

This chronic disease process can be helped by homeopathy using Ruta, Calcarea fluorica and Hekla lava, and the herbal Comfrey, Willow bark, Meadowsweet or Devil's Claw. Acupuncture and LASER treatment may also help (see pages 46–47 and 58–59).

FRACTURES

This term refers to a break or crack in a bone (see page 63). Herbal Comfrey or Boneset and homeopathic Calcarea fluorica, Ruta, Symphytum and Arnica are commonly used as treatment, along with external or internal fixation as necessary.

LAMENESS

This condition arises from any pain in a cat's limb due to arthritis, sprain, strain or trauma, for example, or in the musculature of the shoulder or hip. Sometimes it can be caused by nerve impingement in the neck or lumbar spine. Chiropractic evaluation is important in its treatment. Acupuncture or treatments listed here for the specific problems can help. Cats are forever climbing or jumping onto high perches, resulting in a need to jump down again, and this repetitive trauma to the front limbs can cause lameness.

OSTEOCHONDRITIS DISSECANS (OCD)

This is a disturbance in the cartilage surface of the joint and surgery is often offered for treatment, but your cat may respond to medical input as a first option. Acupuncture, homeopathy using Ruta, Calcarea fluorica, Caulophyllum, Ledum or Kalmia according to the patient, and the herbs Comfrey, Meadowsweet and Cleavers and LASER therapy can be very helpful (see page 59).

OSTEOSARCOMA

This is usually a very painful, aggressive and life-threatening cancer of the bone (see pages 86–87).

RHEUMATISM

This painful muscular disease can be helped in a similar way to arthritis – see Arthritis (opposite) for recommended treatments.

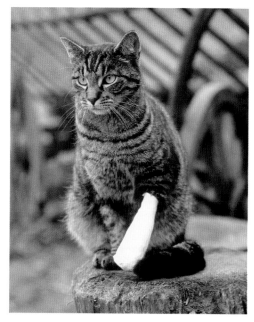

Some form of fixation is often needed for fractures (seek veterinary help).

ROAD TRAFFIC ACCIDENT

Cars commonly collide with cats, or vice versa, and those that survive often suffer lameness or other locomotor issues. It is recommended that any cat involved in a road traffic accident should receive at least a chiropractic check, and if any problem is found, acupuncture and homeopathy can then be used to speed healing (see pages 46–51).

SPRAIN/JOINT INJURY

This injury is an acute form of arthritis involving damage to ligaments and the joint capsule. LASER therapy and homeopathic Ruta are usually the treatments of choice in natural medicine (see page 59). Support bandaging will help if practical. If the joint is very swollen, homeopathic Apis and herbal Dandelion can help to reduce the swelling.

BACK AND NECK PROBLEMS

The development of your cat's skeleton, including the spine of the neck and back, depends upon healthy nutrition and normal growth rate. If growth is too rapid or if there is dietary imbalance or deficiency, this may encourage developmental abnormalities to arise. Seek veterinary help in all cases.

Hypericum perforatum *is a homeopathic medicine used for nerve injury.*

FRACTURES

If your cat suffers a fractured bone, herbal Comfrey (or knitbone) and homeopathic Calcarea fluorica, Ruta, Symphytum and Arnica can be used to aid and speed healing of the fracture, in addition to any fixation of the bone externally or internally as required. In the case of spinal fractures, homeopathic Hypericum can be helpful in limiting nerve damage.

ILIAC THROMBOSIS

This is not in fact a back or neck problem, but can appear superficially similar. Anything that promotes the formation of blood clots in the circulation can lead to iliac thrombosis, cardiomyopathy in older cats being one possible cause. The most likely place for such clots to form is in the arteries supplying the legs. This thrombosis results in severe cramps in the hind leg muscles and often blueing of the legs from the groin down. The cat often loses the use of her hind legs and is found dragging her hind quarters. The outlook is frequently specified as poor, but the author has witnessed full recovery in most cases

under homeopathic treatment and
acupuncture (see pages 46–51).

MISALIGNMENT

Any part of a cat's skeleton can become
misaligned, resulting in malfunction, pain and
muscle spasm. Spinal misalignment is very
common in cats and will impinge on nerve
function, to limbs, muscles or internal organs.
Common sites of problems are the top of the
neck (the atlanto-occipital joint), the lower
neck (where the forelimb nerves emerge),
the thoracolumbar junction and lumbosacral
junction (where the hind limb nerves
emerge). Chiropractic manipulation is
essential, supported by acupuncture, LASER
therapy, physiotherapy and other modalities,
as needed (see pages 46–51). Homeopathic
Arnica, Ruta and Hypericum may also help
with pain control and to stimulate healing.

PARALYSIS (SEE ALSO ILIAC THROMBOSIS OPPOSITE)

Road traffic accidents are the most common
form of injury in cats. Back injury with pain
and often paralysis is quite common. Any
traumatic blow to the spine can cause
fractures or sprains and damage to the spinal
cord. In the short term, oedema, swelling,
inflammation and pain must be reduced.
Steroids and surgical treatment are often
offered in conventional practice. The aim of
natural medicine is to stimulate the healing
of nerves. Results have usually been good in
cases of cats treated with natural medicine
without surgery. Acupuncture is the main
treatment, supported by gentle chiropractic
manipulation, LASER therapy and
homeopathy to control pain, oedema and

Conium maculatum *can be used to treat progressive hind limb weakness.*

tissue damage, and to promote the
subsequent healing of nerves and other
structures and other soft tissues.

Not uncommonly, a cat will experience
paralysis of a forelimb (radial nerve), possibly
from climbing and swinging from the limb,
either accidentally or in order to catch prey. If
the shoulder region is stretched to extremes,
the radial nerve can be damaged. The
recommended treatment is the same as for
back injury (see above). See also Iliac
Thrombosis (see opposite)

WEAKNESS

It is important to distinguish weakness as a
consequence of age-related degeneration
from that of arthritis (see page 68). If your cat
is suffering from age-related weakness, it can
usually be helped by homeopathic Causticum
or Conium.

EYE AND EAR PROBLEMS

Eye problems in your cat can be frightening because of the threat of losing eyesight, but the eye is often observed to heal exceptionally vigorously under homeopathic guidance and stimulus, sometimes aided by herbal treatment or acupuncture. Ear problems are often part of a more general skin problem and can be recognized by discharges, ear scratching or rubbing or a change in ear or head carriage.

Eye injury can lead to cataract formation, which will limit sight in the affected eye.

CATARACT

A rare occurence in cats, this is characterized by progressive opacity of the lens. It can be age related or it can develop as a result of an eye injury. There are also congenital and hereditary cataracts, which are very rare in cats. Homeopathic Calcarea fluorica and Silicea are often used. Calcarea carbonica, Phosphorus and Conium may help age-related cataracts, while Senega may help cataracts following surgery. Age-related 'hardening' (sclerosis) of the lens is treated similarly.

CONJUNCTIVITIS

This condition is recognized by a redness of the soft tissue inside the eyelids, and may come with or without discharge. Homeopathic Aconitum and Argentum nitricum are commonly used in its treatment. Euphrasia may be used homeopathically or herbally, and can be applied to the eye as a lotion. In cats with chlamydia, a nosode (a medicine prepared in the same way as other homeopathic medicines, but using disease material) may be a useful adjunct to treatment, achieving a more permanent clearance (see pages 34–35).

CORNEAL ULCER

This condition can result from injury or infection, and can be very painful. The most common homeopathic treatments are Conium and Mercurius corrosivus, indicated when there is great photophobia (extreme sensitivity to light) and pain. Treatment has usually been very successful. Euphrasia eye lotion may also help, particularly if there is blueing.

EXTERNAL EAR INFLAMMATION (OTITIS EXTERNA)

This sometimes very stubborn condition can usually be helped by natural medicine and management. Homeopathic Calcarea sulphurica, Causticum, Graphites, Kali bichromicum, Kali sulphuricum, Kreosotum, Mercurius solubilis, Psorinum, Pulsatilla, Pyrogenium and Sulphur are commonly used, according to the individual cat's constitution and signs. Homeopathic Belladonna can help acute and painful inflammation. Management can be aided by using dilute aromatherapy oils such as Lavender, Rosemary and Tea tree or by using either boric acid powder or iodoform powder. If there are ear mites, the aforementioned aromatherapy can help. Sparing use of iodoform powder may also help.

GLAUCOMA

This is swelling of the eyeball, usually causing pain. Homeopathic Belladonna, Gelsemium or Spigelia are often used in the natural treatment of this condition. It is rarely seen before conventional drugs have been started, so it is difficult to know whether homeopathy alone can help.

HORNER'S SYNDROME

In this condition the eyeball is pulled back and the third eyelid comes across. The upper eyelid droops, the lower eyelid can be elevated and the pupil is constricted. It results from damage to the sympathetic nerves, sometimes by head or neck injury. Acupuncture supported by homeopathic Physostigminum has helped in some cases, but spontaneous recovery can also occur.

MIDDLE AND INNER EAR INFLAMMATION (*OTITIS MEDIA* AND *OTITIS INTERNA*)

This condition usually results in the cat's head tilting, along with loss of balance. Badly affected cats can roll along the floor. Homeopathic Causticum and Conium usually help to restore more normal function. There may be purulent infection, with which homeopathic Hepar sulphuris can help. Aromatherapy, using Lavender and Rosemary, can also be effective.

PANNUS

The appearance of blood vessels on the cornea, with or without pigmentation, can usually be treated homeopathically using Argentum nitricum, Aurum metallicum, Mercurius solubilis or Silicea, depending upon the individual patient's characteristics.

UVEITIS

This is a deep and painful eye inflammation. Sight and even the eye itself can be lost. Experience has shown that integrated acupuncture and homeopathy using Belladonna, Gelsemium, Phosphorus or Spigelia, depending upon constitutional and local signs, can often save the cat's sight.

CHEST AND HEART PROBLEMS

Maintaining a healthy heart and lungs is vital for the correct circulation of blood and for gaseous exchange. The function of this is to supply the tissues with essential nutrients and oxygen, and to clear away excess carbon dioxide and the potentially toxic by-products of metabolism.

In homeopathic potency, Digitalis helps many different heart problems.

ASCITES

If the right side of the heart of a cat is failing to pump blood sufficiently, fluid can accumulate in the abdomen. Herbal diuretics such as Dandelion leaf can help to clear the fluid, in addition to appropriate homeopathic heart medication (see Heart Disease opposite). Homeopathic medicines that may help are Adonis, Apis, Apocynum and Digitalis.

ASTHMA

Cats with asthma variably show difficulty with breathing, a cough, a 'nasal' sounding voice and bubbly breathing. During an 'attack' they can have blueing on the inside of the mouth. Avoid a cat inhaling cigarette smoke or other irritant fumes and consider aromatherapy using Eucalyptus. Homeopathic treatment has restored a normal life to many cats without resorting to drugs.

COUGH

There are a great many variations of cough and a multitude of conditions that have cough as a symptom or sign. Some common homeopathic medicines that can be helpful are Aconitum (sudden onset and if worse when cold), Antimonium tartaricum (rattling cough), Arsenicum (if worse just after midnight), Bryonia (if worse for movement, eating or drinking), Causticum (if worse on becoming warm), Coccus (with fluid expectoration), Drosera (spasmodic cough and if worse at night), Dulcamara (if worse in damp weather), Ipecacuanha (with vomiting), Mercurius solubilis (if worse in the hours of darkness), Phosphorus (if worse in cold air), Pulsatilla (if worse morning and night and better in fresh air) and Spongia (if resulting from heart disease). The essential oils Cedarwood, Eucalyptus or Hyssop may help coughs. Hairball or worms may cause a cough (see pages 38–39 and 65).

HEART COUGH

If the left side of a cat's heart fails to pump blood properly, a 'heart cough' can result from congestion of the lungs. Bryonia, Digitalis or Spongia are homeopathic medicines that can be helpful, along with herbal diuretic support such as Dandelion leaf.

HEART DISEASE

Experience has shown that homeopathic medication, properly applied, can be very successful in bringing back a good quality of life to many cats suffering chronic heart disease. In many cases, conventional medication has proved unnecessary and in many others it has been possible to reduce conventional medication. However, serious heart problems are not normally suitable for treatment with home medication. Homeopathic medication is extremely unlikely to interfere with any conventional drugs your vet may prescribe for your cat, but it is advisable that you seek the advice of an experienced holistic vet if you wish to use natural medicine, either alone or with conventional medicine. Herbal medicine on the other hand can conflict with conventional

drugs or dangerously summate with them if they contain similar compounds or compounds with a similar action in the body, since material doses are given.

Heart conditions that have been treated with good success are arrhythmia, bradycardia (slow heart), cardiomegaly (enlarged heart), cardiomyopathy (disease of the heart muscle), heart failure (left, right or both), heart murmur (heart valve problems) and tachycardia (fast heart). The following homeopathic medicines are commonly used: Aconitum, Adonis, Apocynum, Arsenicum, Cactus, Carbo vegetabilis, Cinchona, Coffea, Convallaria, Crataegus, Digitalis, Gelsemium, Glonoinum, Kali nitricum, Lachesis, Laurocerasus, Lilium tigrinum, Lycopodium, Lycopus, Naja, Natrum muriaticum, Nux vomica, Phosphorus, Prunus, Spartium, Spigelia, Spongia, Strophanthus, Tabacum and Viscum album. Those with in-depth experience of homeopathy may wish to consult text books on these medicines, to see which may be suitable for their cat, especially if the heart condition has not been controlled by conventional medication.

PULMONARY OEDEMA/PULMONARY CONGESTION

If the affected cat has a cough, homeopathic medicines that can help are listed under Heart Cough above. If the cat has shortness of breath and a craving for fresh air, then Apis and Carbo vegetabilis may be the appropriate homeopathic treatment. If the cat's mouth is open and there is much saliva, Ammonium carbonicum may be helpful. Herbal Dandelion leaf can help to reduce fluid accumulation.

URINARY PROBLEMS

Urinary problems usually result in changes in urine or urination. There may be blood or pus in your cat's urine, or she may experience straining or pain on urination. Urination may be more frequent or involuntary. Should your cat be unable to urinate, this is a medical emergency and may indicate obstruction.

BLADDER STONES (UROLITHIASIS)
This is a disorder of the metabolism, resulting from imbalances in a cat's diet. The crystals that are the basis of bladder stones may be struvite, which develop in alkaline urine and require acidification of the urine to prevent formation, or oxalate, vice versa. Feeding your cat a natural diet is likely to be the best preventative measure (see pages 18–31). However, homeopathic Berberis may help to prevent the formation of new stones and could even help to dissolve those present. Surgery is sometimes necessary, in the first instance, especially in male cats. Herbal Eupatorium purpureum may also be helpful. It is essential that your cat has a good water intake, to maintain the flow of urine.

BLADDER TUMOUR
This condition is very rare in cats (see pages 86–87). Homeopathy may be able to help in cases of malignant bladder tumour, so consult a holistic vet. If there is bleeding from the growth, homeopathic Nitric acid may help.

BLOOD IN URINE (HAEMATURIA)
Blood can appear in the urine from anywhere in the urinary tract, including the kidneys, bladder, ureter, urethra or prostate. If the blood is a result of kidney degeneration, homeopathic Phosphorus is well indicated. If the affected cat produces clotted blood, homeopathic Ipecacuanha may help. If the blood has arisen from cystitis, see below for recommended treatments. If the blood is from a tumour or polyp, see above for treatment advice. If the blood is from the prostate gland, see pages 78–79.

CYSTITIS
This is inflammation of the urinary bladder and usually occurs in conjunction with bacterial infection, so there may be pus. If the affected cat experiences pain and is straining at urination, homeopathic Cantharis may be helpful. Cleavers, Dandelion root, Parsley, Barley water or Cranberry juice are useful herbal preparations that will help to promote bladder health. A good water intake is essential, to maintain urine flow.

FELINE UROLOGICAL SYNDROME (FUS)
This term is used to described a complex of signs of urinary disorder, including cystitis, bladder stones and sabulous plugs. Historically, the incidence of FUS increased with the introduction of dry cat foods, but has since moderated as those foods have been

Changes in urination behaviour necessitate a visit to your vet.

modified. Feeding your cat a fresh diet is a good insurance against such problems.

INCONTINENCE (ENURESIS)
When cats move into old age they can suffer from involuntary urination. Homeopathic Causticum may help to relieve the problem.

KIDNEY FAILURE
Kidney tissue, once lost, cannot be repaired, so this condition is life-threatening. It can be quite advanced before signs – thirst, a characteristic smell and weight loss – begin to show. The affected cat can only survive if there is sufficient viable kidney tissue left at the onset of treatment. Homeopathic medicines such as Carbamide, Kali chloricum, Mercurius solubilis or Phosphorus, prescribed according to the individual cat, have been of

great benefit. Fluid therapy may be essential at the outset of treatment.

POLYURIA
If your cat is urinating more than normal and drinking more, this can be a sign of serious disease, such as diabetes mellitus, diabetes insipidus or Cushing's syndrome. Consult a vet for a diagnosis and see pages 84–85.

SABULOUS PLUGS
These affect mainly male cats, when the urethra can become blocked with matrix material and struvite crystals (see Bladder Stones opposite). Veterinary help will probably be needed but experience suggests that early use of homeopathic Sarsaparilla may release the blockage rapidly, avoiding the need for surgical intervention.

REPRODUCTIVE SYSTEM PROBLEMS

Reproductive problems in cats can result in changes in behaviour, failure to breed, abnormal discharges, irregular female cycles, changes in the mammary glands and, in the case of pyometra (an emergency condition), increased thirst. Abnormalities of cycling and pyometra can only occur in an entire female cat.

A normal litter can consist of up to ten kittens – problems in falling pregnant or giving birth are rare.

BIRTH

Cats can give birth to up to ten kittens, rarely more. It is rare for them to suffer complications, either in giving birth or in mothering. There are many natural medicines, both herbal and homeopathic, that can help in instances of birth complications, but this is the realm of the holistic vet. Homeopathic medicines such as Calcarea phosphorica, Caulophyllum, Cuprum aceticum, Gossypium, Pulsatilla or Secale may be indicated.

'CALLING'

A female cat that has not been spayed will display repeated cycles of oestrus lasting for up to three weeks and at three-week intervals almost throughout the year. In the northern hemisphere, this is usually March to October. A 'calling' cat will make mewling or yowling sounds and will roll about on the floor. This is normal behaviour and will stop if mating occurs. Homeopathic Apis, Lachesis, Lilium tigrinum, Platina or Pulsatilla, prescribed according to the cat's behaviour, will offer help in many cases.

INFERTILITY AND DECREASED LIBIDO
These problems are uncommon in cats but, if they do occur, homeopathic medicines such as Agnus castus, Lachesis, Natrum muriaticum, Pulsatilla or Sepia, prescribed according to the cat's individual characteristics can help in many cases. Diet is a very important consideration in both sexes, since poor nutrition in any form is likely to hit reproduction first.

LACTATION
If the mother cat produces an insufficient amount of milk for her young to suckle, homeopathic Pulsatilla and high-potency Urtica or herbal Milk thistle and Goat's rue can often remedy the situation. Diet is also very important, particularly with regard to the nutritional energy drain represented by lactation. If the mother's milk persists after weaning, low-potency homeopathic Urtica or herbal Dandelion leaf can help to reduce it.

MAMMARY TUMOURS
In cats these are generally malignant (see pages 86–87). In general the surgical removal of malignant tumours can lead to rapid growth of lung secondaries and death within a few months. Benign growths, which are less common in cats, rarely need removal. Spaying is usually recommended (see pages 42–43). While there may be dangers with

performing a biopsy, it is the way your vet can diagnose malignancy in the early stages.

MASTITIS
Inflammation of the mammary glands can occur at any time, but it usually happens either during or after the nursing period. Belladonna (if hot, red and sore), Bryonia (if swollen and painful on movement) and Lachesis (if purpling) have been found useful.

PREGNANCY
Homeopathic Caulophyllum given about six times during the last three weeks of pregnancy is likely to help the subsequent birth process. Homeopathic Calcarea phosphorica given similarly and for the first week after delivery can aid lactation and also the skeletal development and strength of the kittens.

PYOMETRA
This can be an emergency condition and you should seek veterinary help promptly. With the guidance of a holistic vet, homeopathic Aletris, Caulophyllum, Lilium tigrinum or Sepia may help, but if the treatment does not bring rapid relief, surgery will be necessary to prevent serious and life-threatening complications.

A pregnant cat requires extra food and can benefit from skilled homeopathic medication.

OTHER CONDITIONS
BEHAVIOURAL ISSUES

Behaviour is but a mirror of a cat's feelings and emotions, and when observing behaviour the best we can do is guess at the mental process behind it. When behaviour impinges on your cat's enjoyment of life or on your enjoyment of the relationship you have with your cat, a way needs to be sought to modify it for the better.

A GUIDE TO NATURAL REMEDIES FOR BEHAVIOURAL ISSUES

Behavioural issue	Therapies and remedies
Aggression	Homeopathy: Belladonna, Lycopodium, Nitric acid, Nux vomica, Aromatherapy: Lavender, Chamomile, Bach Flowers: Heather, Vervain, Vine, Willow, Herbs: Hops, Skullcap, Valerian
Anxiety	See Timidity below
Bereavement/grief	Homeopathy: Cyclamen, Ignatia, Natrum muriaticum, Phosphoric acid
Coprophagy (eating faeces)	Homeopathy: Hyoscyamus, Sulphur, Veratrum album
Destructiveness	Homeopathy: Belladonna, Chamomilla, Hyoscyamus, Stramonium, Tarentula hispanica, Aromatherapy: Lavender, Chamomile
Excitability	Homeopathy: Belladonna, Hyoscyamus, Ignatia, Magnesium phosphoricum, Pulsatilla, Stramonium, Aromatherapy: Lavender, Chamomile, Herbs: Hops, Skullcap, Valerian
Fears	Homeopathy: noise fear – Borax, Nitric acid, Nux vomica, Phosphorus; anticipatory – Argentum nitricum, Gelsemium, Lycopodium, Silicea; motion – Bryonia; touch – Arnica, Chamomilla, Lachesis, Nux vomica; thunder – Borax, Gelsemium, Natrum carbonicum, Phosphorus, Rhododendron, Theridion, Aromatherapy: Lavender, Lemon balm, Bach Flowers: Aspen, Mimulus, Rock rose, Herbs: Hops, Skullcap, Valerian
Hyperactivity	Homeopathy: Arsenicum, Coffea, Ignatia, Aromatherapy: Lavender, Chamomile, Herbs: Hops, Skullcap, Valerian
Indifference	Homeopathy: Natrum muriaticum, Platina, Sepia, Bach Flowers: Clematis, Wild rose

Cats can be very territorial animals and will defend their ground aggressively.

Behavioural issue	Therapies and remedies
Jealousy	Homeopathy: Apis, Hyoscyamus, Lachesis, **Bach Flowers:** Holly
Panic	Homeopathy: Aconitum, Gelsemium, Stramonium, **Aromatherapy:** Lavender, **Bach Flowers:** Rock rose, Rescue remedy, **Herbs:** Hops, Skullcap, Valerian
Rage	Homeopathy: Belladonna, Hyoscyamus, Lyssin, Stramonium, **Aromatherapy:** Lavender, **Bach Flowers:** Holly, Vine, **Herbs:** Hops, Skullcap, Valerian
Resentment	Homeopathy: Natrum muriaticum, Staphisagria, **Bach Flowers:** Willow
Restlessness	Homeopathy: Arsenicum, Coffea, Ignatia, Rhus toxicodendron, Stramonium, **Aromatherapy:** Lavender, Camomile, **Bach Flowers:** Impatiens, Vervain, **Herbs:** Hops
Separation anxiety	Homeopathy: Lycopodium, Phosphorus, Pulsatilla, **Aromatherapy:** Lemon balm, **Bach Flowers:** Aspen, Cerato, Larch, Mimulus
Stress	Homeopathy: Natrum muriaticum, Nux vomica, Staphisagria, **Aromatherapy:** Lavender, Lemon balm, Jasmine, **Bach Flowers:** Holly, Mimulus, Walnut, **Herbs:** Hops, Passiflora, Skullcap, Valerian
Timidity/lacking confidence	Homeopathy: Ignatia, Natrum muriaticum, Pulsatilla, Silicea, **Aromatherapy:** Lavender, Lemon balm, **Bach Flowers:** Larch, Mimulus, Vervain
Urine spraying (inappropriate)	Homeopathy: Cantharis, Natrum muriaticum, Staphisagria, Stramonium, **Bach Flowers:** Willow
Wandering/roaming	Homeopathy: Bryonia, Sulphur, Tuberculinum bovinum

ALLERGY AND ATOPY

Allergy or atopy result from immune disturbance, which can be caused by chemicals, viruses and vaccination. If this disturbance is corrected, allergy will fade and the signs and symptoms subside. Allergy is common in cats and usually expresses itself in the skin or the respiratory system. The approach of holistic and natural medicine to the problem differs to that commonly recommended by conventional vets.

THE UNDERLYING ISSUE

The term 'allergy' is derived from the ancient Greek meaning 'other function', referring to the incorrect function of the immune system. It is therefore one of the few modern disease names that accurately and meaningfully describes the fundamental problem, rather than simply describing signs and symptoms.

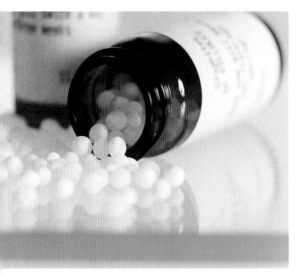

Graphites is one of many homeopathic medicines that may be able to help in cases of allergic skin disease.

Atopy is a term used to describe a generalized allergic or hyperallergic condition.

WHAT TRIGGERS ALLERGIC REACTION?

In allergy the immune system responds inappropriately to 'allergens', which are external materials that trigger the reaction. These may be pollens, house dust, gluten, flea saliva, moulds, grass proteins, plants, food components, nickel, household reagents, agrochemicals or certain other chemicals. A common sign is itchiness of the skin, but diarrhoea, vomiting or respiratory problems (asthma or chronic obstructive pulmonary disease or COPD) are also seen quite regularly (see pages 64–67 and 74–75).

Removing or reducing these allergens from the environment or diet of the cat may temporarily reduce the symptoms, but will not effect a 'cure'. It has to be a lifelong endeavour, which is a daunting prospect. Furthermore, if the allergen is an environmental factor, such as house dust, this would be an impractical option. If it were possible to separate your cat completely from the suspected allergen, the immune disturbance that gives rise to allergy can allow a new allergy to develop to other environmental items. The underlying immune malfunction must be corrected before the cat can be free of allergies. Any powerful immune challenges that are capable of perverting immune function and balance, such as viruses or immunization (vaccines), are likely candidates to cause allergy and revaccination of an allergic cat is certainly not recommended (see pages 32–35).

Desensitizing vaccines may be offered conventionally, which are based on the result of specific allergy tests. This expensive technique seems to be aimed at 'tiring', 'exhausting' or 'wearing out' the immune system into non-reactivity, but only appears to help in a few cases.

TREATING THE NATURAL WAY

Rather than trying to exhaust the immune system or to suppress the allergic reaction with anti-inflammatory drugs like steroids (cortisone) or with antihistamines for life, which can result in deepening of the underlying disease, natural medicine (particularly the homeopathic constitutional approach) can bring about a lasting rebalancing of immune function and cessation of allergy. This requires skilled constitutional prescribing.

It is wise to try to reduce the environmental challenge in the meantime, but whereas in conventional medicine this is a permanent requirement, in natural medicine a normal tolerance for the allergen may be re-established.

HOMEOPATHIC MEDICINES FOR ALLERGIC CATS

The following homeopathic medicines are frequently used in the treatment of allergic cats, prescribed by a holistic vet on the basis of the individual feline patient's characteristics.

Bacillinum
Calcarea carbonica
Graphites
Kali sulphuricum
Natrum muriaticum
Phosphorus
Psorinum
Pulsatilla
Sepia
Sulphur
Thuja
Tub. bov.

The 'bowel nosode' Morgan Bach is also commonly used.

Diet is an essential component of holistic treatment, in that the immune system should heal much faster and more effectively if your cat is given a natural, healthy, unprocessed and species-suitable diet. Furthermore, some allergies occur to dietary chemicals, for which your cat has no need and which may be harmful in any case. A natural diet avoids this hazard.

AUTOIMMUNE AND ENDOCRINE DISORDERS

Autoimmune disorders are those in which the cat's immune system has mis-recognized its own body tissues as 'enemy' and causes them damage. Many different conditions come under this umbrella heading, and most of the endocrine disorders that cats suffer may also be autoimmune in nature. While a poor prognosis is usually offered for these conditions, many cats have recovered well on homeopathic treatment.

A natural, fresh, organic diet is a good adjunct to natural treatment.

virus or vaccine and, at the same time, encounters animal tissue, which can then become confused with the infection, thus sensitizing the immune system to the combined perceived threat. Virus challenge, vaccination and dietary anomalies may therefore give rise to an autoimmune condition. As vaccines often contain residues of animal tissues, it is not impossible that they may provoke a wayward immune response or recognition malfunction of this nature in some cats (see pages 32–35).

Autoimmune syndromes in cats include pemphigus, lupus, eosinophilic dermatitis, miliary dermatitis, thyroid disease and rodent ulcer. Stomatitis, gingivitis and diabetes mellitus may also have autoimmune origins.

WHY AUTOIMMUNITY OCCURS

While actual causes have not been established for certain, it is thought that factors that can impinge on immune function are likely to be involved. This may happen when the body is under attack from, say,

ALTERNATIVES TO CONVENTIONAL TREATMENTS

In conventional practice, immunosuppression is usually considered, by means of high doses and prolonged courses of steroid (cortisone), but this treatment is not without dangers.

Problem	Homeopathic medicine
Addison's disease – insufficiency of the adrenal cortex	Adrenalin, Arsenicum, Phosphorus
Cushing's syndrome – overactive anterior pituitary gland or gland cortex, or both	ACTH, Adrenal sarcode, Natrum muriaticum, Pituitary sarcode, Quercus robur
Diabetes insipidus – increased thirst most commonly from underactivity of the posterior pituitary gland	Acetic acid, Argentum metallicum, Aurum muriaticum, Phosphoric acid, Phosphorus
Diabetes mellitus – reduced ability of the pancreas to produce insulin for correct sugar metabolism	Arsenicum, Insulin, Phosphorus, Syzigium, Uranium nitricum
Hyperthyroidosis – overactive thyroid gland	Arsenicum, Iodum, Phosphorus, Thyroid sarcode (high potency)
Hypothyroidosis – underactive thyroid gland	Calcarea carbonica, Iodum, Thyroid sarcode (low potency)

Many cases appear to respond very positively to homeopathic treatment with holistic support in the shape of a natural, fresh, organic diet. At least, recovery is coincidental with homeopathic input. These successful cases appear to show that homeopathy can provide a realistic alternative to suppressive drug therapy. The approach used is the homeopathic constitutional one, tailored to the individual cat rather than to the name of the disease, which is best delivered by a holistic vet. Many cases on record seem to have enjoyed apparent cure, defying the poor prognosis that is usually offered.

ENDOCRINE DISORDERS AND TREATMENT

Apart from those of the ovaries or testes (see pages 78–79), the endocrine disorders that can occur in cats are Addison's disease (Hypoadrenocorticism), Cushing's syndrome (Hyperadrenocorticism), diabetes insipidus, diabetes mellitus, hyperthyroidosis and hypothyroidosis. In the case of most of these conditions, there are clues that there may be an autoimmune component. As more research unfolds, this suspicion may in time be confirmed.

There are homeopathic (see the panel above), dietary and herbal means of treating these disorders, with reasonable hopes of positive results. These should be administered under the care of a holistic vet. The immune and endocrine systems are central to control of the body's internal balance, so optimal health depends upon their correct function.

CANCER – AN APPRAISAL

Cancer is a common serious disease, with one in three cats in the USA expected to develop it, and it appears to have become more prevalent over the years. No particular reason for this has been agreed upon, but diet, vaccination, chemicals and environmental degradation are possible players. An encouraging number of cases have recovered while using holistic and natural medicine.

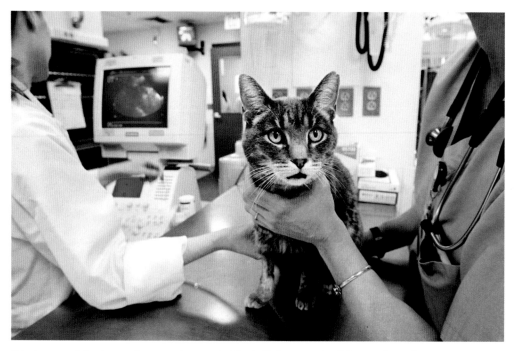

Veterinary medicine has made many advances, but the holistic approach still has much to offer.

HOW AND WHY IT OCCURS

Cancer is a disease in which certain cells grow and multiply in a way that is outside the body's normal hierarchical control. This can either result in growths – tumours – that are capable of spreading, known as metastasis, causing damage or even proving fatal in malignant types, or it can affect the blood or the lymphatic system. Cancer is very prevalent in cats, with no breed appearing to have a particular susceptibility, although white cats are more vulnerable to skin cancer.

Some causative factors that appear to have been identified from past cases are injury and trauma, whether mental or physical, chemical exposure, so-called 'electro-magnetic smog', incorrect diet, viruses and vaccination. These factors may act singly or together. In this connection, it is interesting and concerning to note that many living vaccines are cultured on laboratory cell cultures that intentionally contain cancer DNA. In cats there is a known risk of cancer developing at the site of injection, possibly for this very reason. In the USA a vaccine-site tumour, vaccination-associated fibrosarcoma (VAS), is well known, affecting up to one in a thousand vaccinated cats.

CONVENTIONAL AND HOLISTIC APPROACHES

Surgery, chemotherapy, radiotherapy, steroid treatment or various combinations of these are usually offered conventionally. If the tumour is malignant and invasive, surgical removal may lead to the 'release' and rapid development of secondary growths that may already have started in a very small way. Particular examples are osteosarcoma and mammary carcinoma, in which secondary development (mostly in the lungs) is a frequent sequel to surgery. Not all types of cancer are considered amenable to chemotherapy. You are advised to seek the expert advice of a specialist if considering this route. Interestingly, chemotherapy is not usually taken as badly by feline patients as it is by humans, but nonetheless there are usually harmful side effects and some sensitive cats can be made very miserable.

In holistic medicine we believe that if the body has the power and will to fight the cancer, and if its ability is appropriately

stimulated (for example by homeopathy) and all obstacles to recovery are removed, then a positive outcome can follow. This is borne out in real-life experience by a number of cases. While by no means all cases end well, recoveries have been recorded in most types of cancer. These include fibrosarcoma, osteosarcoma, mast cell tumour, histiocytoma, lymphoma, mammary carcinoma, liver cancer and spindle cell tumour. It even appears from experience that, contrary to popularly held belief, homeopathy can still exert benefit even in the face of chemotherapy or steroid treatment. This means that you do not have to adopt a strictly 'either/or' approach. It is recommended that any alternative medical treatment is given by a holistic vet.

If not already adhering to one, a change to a healthy, natural, fresh, organic and species-suitable diet is an essential component of the holistic approach.

REASONS FOR HOPE

A positive outcome is not an impossible target with cancer and there are grounds for reasonable hope, with recovery occurring in a significant number of cases. However, it is clear that cancer remains a particularly vicious and powerful enemy to cats. In order to avoid additional anxiety and disappointment, the prognosis offered at the outset of treatment of any single case must therefore be very guarded. A great deal of work needs to be done to establish methods of prevention. The author believes that a holistic and natural lifestyle is the best way to ensure optimum health and therefore of diminishing the risk of serious disease.

THE OLDER CAT

Just because a cat has reached old age does not mean that she cannot continue to enjoy life. So beware of any tendency you may have to sideline your ageing cat and reduce her activity and interaction to a level below that which she is capable of achieving. The pride, dignity and demeanour of older cats makes them very special.

Older cats can continue to enjoy their lives and remain agile and healthy until they die.

THE AGEING PROCESS

There is no such disease as 'old age' – age is simply an accident of time. Only if a cat's constitution is not in balance does her in-built healing capability deteriorate with age. So there is no rule that states that an older cat must suffer more disease or that says she cannot die healthy when the time comes. The natural ageing process of degeneration should not cause significant malfunction. The fact that our culture appears to accept that disease is inevitable in the aged is a sad comment on health management.

PREVENTING PROBLEMS

As Irish playwright George Bernard Shaw famously observed, 'We don't stop playing because we grow old; we grow old because we stop playing', so you must consider ways of preventing 'old age' diseases while your cat is young. Diet and lifestyle are both important factors, and feeding your cat a fresh, healthy diet with bones to chew will benefit skeletal and dental health. If you avoid over-vaccinating your cat (see pages 32–35), provide her with a loving and happy home and attend to any injuries promptly with natural healing methods in an effort to

The older cat has great dignity and presence and is deserving of special care.

prevent later complications, you will very likely be rewarded with a healthy, active and fun-loving pet in old age. With the appropriate diet and oral care, your cat should keep her teeth and not require dental intervention (see pages 17–19).

If your cat has reached older age with many health problems, because you did not know how to, or were not able to, take such preventative measures when she was younger, it may not be too late to act. The body retains healing capacity up until death. It is true that you may not see a full recovery in your pet, since the healing processes may be slower or incomplete. But you should be able to initiate a reversal process, that will restore enough of your cat's health to make life a lot more enjoyable and worthwhile.

THE SIGNS OF WEAR AND TEAR

When the above ideal strategy or situation fails, you will notice your older cat's coat losing its shine and she may lose a lot of weight. Her eyes may grow dimmer from degeneration of the lens or cornea or both, leading to reduced visual clarity, and she may show decreased hearing capability. Your elderly cat may suffer arthritis, which can lead to serious mobility problems and can be very painful. Legs can weaken, leading to difficulty in rising from lying and making progress slow. The kidneys may deteriorate, leading to a urine-like smell. Your ageing cat's heart may become weaker, leading to reduced exercise tolerance and activity. Some older cats may suffer urine or faecal incontinence, or it may just be a case of decreased awareness leading to 'accidents'. Obviously, your cat should not be punished for this happening.

Cancer is prevalent in cats (see pages 86–87), and older cats may be more prone to this group of diseases.

BENEFICIAL TREATMENTS

Homeopathy, herbs, acupuncture, chiropractic manipulation, physiotherapy and other therapeutic interventions can supply your elderly cat with effective support, providing an invaluable extension to her active and enjoyable life.

In homeopathy, Rhus toxicodendron 6c twice daily may help the stiffness that worsens in cold damp weather, is worse on rising and eases off with a little exercise.

Minced nettles can form part of a holistic diet programme.

Causticum is a wonderful 'older cat' remedy, which suits stiffness that is worse in cold, bright weather and better in warm and damp conditions. It also has strong indications in the weakness that some older cats suffer and it may help with age-related deafness or the tendency to incontinence. Baryta carbonica can suit your old cat if she has become confused and 'absent'. Ambra grisea is well suited to general ageing and weariness. If your cat experiences heart problems, consider Crataegus in 'mother tincture' form as a first-line of treatment and vitamin E may also help. In kidney disease, which is very common in older cats, Mercurius solubilis, Phosphorus or Kali chloricum may be needed. If your cat's hind legs are giving way, with no obvious pathology and no X-ray signs, then Conium can prove useful.

In herbal medicine, Hawthorn berry can support the heart and Dandelion leaf is a great stand-by as a herbal diuretic. Willow bark, Nettles, Devil's claw, Meadowsweet and Cleavers can help with arthritis and limb problems.

Regular chiropractic checks will help to keep your older cat's musculoskeletal system aligned and prevent back pain (see pages 56–57).

Regular acupuncture can provide immense benefit for your aged cat, acting as a general balancer or helping with medical problems such as back pain, arthritis or paralysis (see pages 46–47).

Should cancer develop (see pages 86–87), it is not impossible for your elderly cat to recover, given the help of homeopathy, herbs and an appropriate diet. While overall statistical results of such treatments are not

Life is for enjoyment and fulfilment, right to the end.

good, cases of recovery from most forms of malignant cancer have been recorded.

The above is a concise guide to treatments only (see also pages 62–79 for more extensive advice on specific common ailments), and it is advisable to seek the advice of a holistic vet for in-depth help with any specific age-related problems.

A FITTING FINALE

In the evening of life it is inevitable that there is a risk of death, which, paradoxical though it may seem, is a natural part of life. We must not begrudge our dear animal companions their departure from life and we must not stand in their way. In a really healthy body, death appears to be organized just as well as living is. Thankfully, a great many aged cats find their own way out, in a time, place and manner of their own choosing. Extremely sad though it is to lose them, how comforting it is to know that they did not die a minute before they wished and did not suffer the so-called 'agonies' of death. We should strive to ensure that our modern lifestyle, diet and management culture does not interfere with the chance of this natural and pain-free exit for our beloved feline companions. We should also be careful to give our cats, which may consider themselves our guardians, formal permission to 'leave'. However, we have also to be alive to the possibility of the need to intervene with euthanasia (see pages 92–93) should the natural process not occur smoothly and humanely. Veterinary guidance is recommended.

EUTHANASIA

It is not unusual for a cat that has been raised, fed and managed according to holistic and natural principles to find her own way out of life, with dignity and peace. If, for some reason, her quality of life has become a burden and it proves impossible for her to make her departure in peace and comfort, some sort of intervention becomes a duty.

A NATURAL END

Death does not necessarily have to involve suffering; after all, it is a natural and inevitable part of every life. Our modern society has made death a mysterious subject and it tends to be taboo to talk about it or to consider it. This is clearly erroneous since it is the only certain event in life, after birth. It would seem that a cat that has enjoyed holistic care throughout her life has an increased chance of a natural end. The body's normal processes are allowed to function in an optimum way. In this way, death happens as part of a natural process and according to the cat's choice of timing and circumstance. This sequence of events happily removes the responsibility of decision from us and would appear to be infinitely the preferred route out of this life for our beloved cat companions, among friends and at home.

MAKING THE RIGHT DECISION

In other, less fortunate situations towards the end of a cat's life, the difficult question of euthanasia arises. All cats are entitled to dignity and comfort, and there are times when, in order to preserve these life qualities,

it may be necessary to 'help your old friend on her way'. Because it is possible to 'put her out of her misery', however, does not always make it the right thing to do.

One course of action to consider, if circumstances are appropriate, is to administer homeopathic medications that can help a cat to make up her mind whether to go or stay – ask your holistic vet for advice. Giving these preparations to your cat does not constitute euthanasia, but helps resolve the 'agonies of indecision' that seem to beset some unfortunate cats in their last hours, days or weeks. This medication can prompt her either to pick up in health and energy or to decide to leave, in which case a peaceful passing is often possible to achieve.

Decisions on whether to perform euthanasia or not are very difficult, and there may not even be a right answer. Clearly, no one wishes to rob an animal of life if it is wrong to do so. Judgment when the correct time has come is highly complex and individual. You may need the help of family, friends, other cat owners and your veterinarian. However, in general if a cat is

Just because a cat is very old and a little infirm, that does not necessitate euthanasia.

suffering significant loss of quality of life such that life holds no attractions for her and if there is no hope for recovery, and if she appears unable to find her own way out calmly and with dignity, then intervention becomes necessary. Signs to watch for in your cat are loss of interest in surroundings and lack of reactivity, but if your cat is actively engaging in her environment and taking an active interest in what is going on, it is probably too soon to consider euthanasia.

In all cases where euthanasia is being considered, you are likely to find your vet sympathetic and willing to talk through the situation, to help you in coming to the right decision. Neither vet nor owner would want to take a life incorrectly, so joint discussions are a support to both at such difficult times.

When a decision has been made to perform euthanasia, vets will often make a house call, if possible, to allow a cat to die in her own home among friends. Sedatives may be given beforehand, if it seems appropriate to do so. A lethal injection may then be given, usually into the bloodstream via a vein. Circumstances should be arranged so that this is not a stressful process.

A FINAL RESTING PLACE

When your old feline friend has passed away, there is the practical question of what to do with her body. Burial at home is chosen by many cat owners, and cremation appears to be the other best option. This can be arranged through your vet, so that it can be a dignified and ethical procedure.

INDEX

ACKNOWLEDGEMENTS

PUBLISHER'S ACKNOWLEDGEMENTS

Executive Editor: Trevor Davies
Senior Editor: Charlotte Macey
Deputy Creative Director: Karen Sawyer
Designer: Janis Utton
Picture Library Manager: Jennifer Veall
Picture Researcher: Emma O'Neill
Senior Production Controller: Amanda Mackie

PICTURE ACKNOWLEDGEMENTS

Alamy/David Askham 25; /Adam Burton 89; /DBURKE 58; /Tony Foggon 90; /imagebroker/Reinhard Hölzl 44; /Christophe Laguigné 4; /Premaphotos 41; /Adrian Sherratt 72; /tbkmedia.de 55; /Top-Pics TBK 68; /Ian West 78; /Westend61 GmbH/Creativ Studio Heinemann 49; /Julie Woodhouse 24. Ardea/Jean Michel Labat 19, 64. Corbis/Fotofeeling/Westend61 81; /Radius Images 34; /Hans Reinhard 69. Dorling Kindersley/Tracy Morgan 56. Fotolia/diefotomacher 59; /EcoView 8; /Elenathewise 23 bottom, 47; /iwikoz6 39; /Paylessimages 84; /Sophia Winters 22. GAP Photos/Jonathan Buckley 20; /Keith Burdett 54. Getty Images/Jessica Boone 37; /GK Hart/Vikki Hart 11; /John Kelly 12; /Dave King 1; /Ryan/Beyer 88; /SambaPhoto/Paulo Fridman 7; /traumlichtfabrik 42. Nature Picture Library/Jane Burton 10, 79; /Ulrike Schanz 46; /Mark Taylor 36. Octopus Publishing Group 21 top; /Jane Burton 15, 16, 17, 33, 60, 65; /Ruth Jenkinson 52; /William Lingwood 29; /Lis Parsons 23 top; /William Reavell 31; /Gareth Sambidge 21 bottom. Photolibrary Group/Garden Photo World/Georgianna Lane 53; /Garden Picture Library/Chris Burrows 70; /Garden Picture Library/Mark Turner 48; /imagebroker RF/Konrad Wothe 32; /Juniors Bildarchiv 13, 66; /Oxford Scientific (OSF)/London Scientific Films 38; /Peter Arnold Images/Ed Reschke 74. Press Association Images/Steven Senne/AP 86. RSPCA/61, /Mike Lane 91. Science Photo Library/Gustoimages 82. Still Pictures/WILDLIFE/D.Harms 71. SuperStock/age fotostock 2, 93. Warren Photographic/Jane Burton 14, 77.